D1228427

The Immigrant Heritage of America Series
Cecyle S. Neidle, Editor

How The Irish Became Americans

By JOSEPH P. O'GRADY

La Salle College

TWAYNE PUBLISHERS
A DIVISION OF G. K. HALL & CO., BOSTON

To

Joseph Patrick, Jr., Karen Marie, Noreen,
Michelle, and Michael Justin; may
they never forget their past as
they continue this story.

Preface

RESTING, as this study does, upon years of reading, research, and reflection, it satisfies a long-standing desire to sum up my understanding of what it was like to be Irish in America during the last three hundred years. As a summary, it will not give the complete story. No survey does, but hopefully the reader will find here the historical outline that describes a people forced to live in a new, alien, and somewhat unreceptive world. Based on the firm conviction that minority groups in America function as successful pressure groups only when they possess a cause around which they can rally their people, the bulk of this study will focus upon that issue—the Anglo-Irish struggle. One will find descriptions of how events in Ireland and England created the Anglo-Irish struggle, the forces that drove the Irish to America and that formed a new Irish nation here, how this new nation influenced the old struggle, and how that struggle conditioned the Irishman's life in America. The book will flow from one side of the Atlantic to the other and emphasize how events on one side influenced those on the other. It will close rapidly after the end of the Anglo-Irish struggle, as Irish-Americans, henceforth without the cause that had given them cohesiveness, rapidly merged into the population and became Americans of Irish descent.

To the extent that this book tells its story, some will consider it successful. Yet, because it will make no attempt to tell the full story, it will fail to recapture the human quality that made the experiences of the Irish immigrant real and dynamic—the human ingredients that continue to make their story meaningful to anyone who wishes to learn about a people on the road from oppression to freedom. That kind of awareness comes from careful reading of Irish and Irish-American poetry and literature. The author would urge anyone who wishes to acquire that understanding to devote some time to such reading. In that way the reader will add sensitivity to the outline found here and gain a more complete view of what it was like to be Irish in America.

The author would like to express his appreciation to the many people who have enlivened his interest in Irish studies: to his father, now gone twenty-two years, from whom he first learned about Irish politics and about such figures as Eamon de Valera; to his mother who retains that priceless view of life so characteristic of her Irish past, undiluted after forty years in America; to Professor Thomas N. Brown who first raised the author's interest in Irish life to the level of serious study; to the authors who have preserved Ireland's and America's past; to the numerous librarians and their institutions who have extended a welcome to him in the past fifteen years; to Miss Georgette Most, who for years has patiently collected his materials; to Mrs. Cecyle S. Neidle, the thoughtful editor who first suggested this book; to three student assistants, Rich Remer, Gene Gallagher, and Mary Ann Butler, for their constant assistance; to Mrs. Madeleine Flounders who typed many of these thoughts in different forms; to Mrs. Clare McCarthy and my sister, Sister Marie Teresé, for the typing of the final drafts; and last, but far from least, to my wife who continues to be a source of inspiration both to me and our children.

Newtown Square, Pennsylvania

Prologue

America as a Pluralistic Society

IN their search for an understanding of America, historians have formed many schools of thought, but most of those who have attempted an explanation of her democratic impulse have found their inspiration in the forces of either heredity, or environment, or both.

The heredity school began, on the professional level at least, with Professor Herbert Baxter Adams who formed his ideas while studying for a doctoral degree in Germany in the latter half of the nineteenth century. Concerned with the evolution of political institutions, he accepted the German thesis that the seeds of Western democratic institutions first appeared among Germanic tribes. In that re-created past of the Teutonic forest, Adams found the origins of parliamentary institutions, trial by jury, and other democratic practices; but he went much further on his return to the United States, when he taught that America itself developed from such "germs" and that she owed her institutions to the miraculous work of heredity.

Meanwhile, young Frederick Jackson Turner, born on the frontier earned his bachelor's and master's degrees at the University of Wisconsin and traveled to Johns Hopkins for his doctor's degree. There he discovered in Professor Adams' "von Ranke-type seminar" that America owed her democracy to the Teutonic forests. The encounter produced a mild convulsion which emerged publicly at the 1893 Chicago meeting of the American Historical Association, when Turner read his now-famous paper, "The Significance of the Frontier in American History." Turner did not deny the dream of his mentor, but he did revolt against the exclusive emphasis on the Teutonic origins, for he found the key that unlocked the door to the American past, not in the Germanic forest, but in the American forest; not in the Germanic frontier, but in the American frontier;

not in America's hereditary influences, but in America's environment.

Turner reflected his age and his world, and his thesis touched on both the growing nationalism of America and the increasing emphasis by intellectuals upon environment and change. Because it did, his theory dominated twentieth-century American historiography. Hundreds of students struggled both for and against the frontier thesis until in the 1950's the majority accepted the belief that both heredity and environment contributed to the emergence of American democracy. Individuals undeniably arrived with certain ideas, but the frontier influenced their lives from the start by permitting them to manipulate these ideas without the restrictions imposed by monarchy, hereditary aristocracy, established church, or any other social institution.

If consensus characterized the historiography of the 1950's, discontent characterized the thinking of the 1960's, and no longer can one find any generally held belief concerning the origin of American democracy. In fact, some historians no longer seek to discover what made America a great democracy; instead, they seek to find what made it the opposite. They find no idealism in America's foreign policy, but only the self-interest of selfish men. In short, they ignore the good in America's past to focus on the evil.

As the 1960's drew to a close, it seemed clear that the disruptions that occurred in all walks of American life during that decade had caused some serious soul-searching and significant reforms. The confrontations over race, the war in Vietnam, government priorities, education, ecology, and other issues have forced open many doors to many insights in all fields. Sociologists, for instance, have discovered that the Negro drive for equality and integration, which has characterized much of American life since the end of World War II, in turn stimulated the reemergence of ethnic consciousness. This in turn caused the demise of the "melting pot" theory of American life during the 1960's and the gradual emergence in a belief that only in the interplay of group relations can one define and solve the problems that face America today and in the foreseeable future.

Insights such as these cannot but help to influence the historians' view of the past. In fact, the debates of the 1960's have clearly created the need for a new view of the American past. The next generation cannot find its understanding of America's democracy in either hereditary or in environmental forces, or in a combination of both; in either the German or American forests; in what the settlers brought here or what they found here. Yet, in this author's opinion they will find an acceptable understanding of the origin, meaning, and purpose of American democracy in the study of how Americans, operating in groups, forced the nation to fulfill the needs of its citizens.

From the start, America has been a nation of groups. Individuals act within the confines of their groups to define their own needs; then by group action they attempt to influence the institutions of society. Too, America has always rested upon the belief that the nation must respond to the needs of the people, yet this has been difficult to achieve precisely because each group defines its needs differently and each uses whatever means exist to bring its demands to those in office. In this context the politician must reconcile the different demands into some kind of acceptable consensus. This concept of American life forces the historian to conclude that American democracy rests upon nothing more than a series of demands, postulated as needs by different groups, to which the government must respond and the reduction of these various demands by the politician to a consensus acceptable to the majority. Thus, the historian must study the action of individuals and groups as America grew not from what people thought, but from what they did.

Future historians, quite obviously, will not ignore the factors of heredity that Adams favored or the factors of environment that Turner listed, for both made meaningful contributions to the context of life in which these groups acted. It does mean, however, that one can no longer emphasize either one or the other or a combination of both. In effect, the people of America did not bring their democracy with them, nor did they find it here. They made it from the interaction of many ideas and interests as defined by many groups. The clash of these ideas generated pressures upon both individuals and groups to make decisions that in turn simply created new demands from new groups. In that momentum one finds the origin, meaning, and purpose of America. Born into a world of pluralism, Americans learned by trial and error how to satisfy the needs and interests of her many groups.

Into that kind of a world the Irish came and contributed to the growth of that kind of America. They did not forget their past as the following pages will show. In fact, their memory and involvement with Irish events gave them the cohesiveness necessary for their role in politics, which, in turn, created the conditions necessary for their assimilation in American society. By remaining involved in Irish affairs, they became Americans.

Contents

CHAPTER 1

Pains of Irish Life

I   Medieval Years

IRELAND, like Poland, stands on the edge of Europe, the product of a geographic sleight-of-hand that placed her far enough from continental Europe to insure her relative isolation until the middle of the sixteenth century. As a result, by the time she entered the mainstream of European political development, she had her own customs and traditions; and her people guarded these with fierce jealousy through the centuries that followed.

However, Ireland did not stand so far beyond Europe's limits as to avoid all contacts. Her nearness to England meant that most of those influences would come from that direction. This second aspect of her geography, proximity to England, profoundly influenced her history, for it denied the Irish, no matter how hard they tried, real freedom. It does so no less today. In short, Ireland's position on the globe paradoxically encouraged provincialism on one hand; on the other, it created a relationship with England which weakened that aspect of Ireland's national life and even her status as an independent nation.

Geography's internal influence also moved Ireland in the direction of localism. Harsh mountains and rocky highlands cover one eighth of the island, and in these areas one can cultivate only coarse grass, which is good only for rough grazing at best. Small but sharp and steep foothills or drumlins cover another significant piece of the island, while the famous peat bogs further reduce the amount of productive soil to about 50 percent of the land surface.

Geography thus influenced Ireland by placing her on the edge of Europe, but close to England, and by creating internal divisions to make conquest beyond the small eastern region centering on Dublin a task which few attempted and no one accomplished. It also contributed to Ireland's ability, in spite of her harsh world, to conquer those who came to conquer her. The newcomer quickly merged with the past, and that fierce sense of independence which belonged to the old became characteristic of the new.[1]

Ireland's relationship to Europe and England clearly existed from the start. Her first people, basically hunters, made the trip to Ireland by way of the land marshes that connected Denmark to England and then to Ireland by way of the Irish Sea. Knowledge of agriculture and the more settled ways of farmers passed along the same path from the heart of continental Europe to the forests of Ireland. Then sometime after 600 B.C. the Celts landed in Ireland.[2]

The Celts possessed a long tradition of domination over Central and Western Europe. Both Greek and Roman generals had cause to fear these warriors, and neither pretended to dispute Celtic power for many years. The Celts brought to Ireland a language, a skill in ironworking, and an interest in agricultural development. Under their influence Irish life became somewhat more stabilized, and kingdoms appeared as leadership fell from the hands of purely military men into those who farmed as well as fought. This reorganization of the nation's power permitted the Celts to limit Roman expansion and thus guaranteed the development of Ireland free of Roman influences.

Ireland's geographic position had helped the Celts exclude the Romans; but neither it, nor they, could bar Western civilization forever. Interestingly, that influence came more from the efforts of churchmen than from politicians.

In this large area of relatively harsh soil, farming remained difficult and life a bitter reality well into the 19th century. Coupled with a damp climate, these factors discouraged habitation. Hard work and the necessity to escape from reality by enjoying the few advantages that existed filled the lives of the farmers. At the same time, these conditions produced a people who saw in God and a belief in the hereafter the only hope of the future.

The Irish have always been a friendly, but a suspicious people, the latter again the result of geography. The combination of highlands, drumlins, bogs, and mountains discouraged travel and reduced communications to an absolute minimum until well into the modern era. Lack of intercourse only increased the Irish tendency toward localism and limited movement from section to section to only the few.

At the same time, these geographic formations clearly separated Northern Ireland from the rest of the country and the poor West from the rich East, which was situated along the Irish Sea from Dundalk to a point just south of Dublin and inland to a depth of twenty to forty miles. This eastern area formed the heart of Ireland's wealth and greatly influenced her history. Many of the great battles were fought there; her institutions developed there, including the city of Dublin (and all that it means to Irish history). Outsiders came to this area for the rich soil, and because it faced the Irish Sea it virtually invited invaders from England and lands beyond. Once such invaders arrived, however, they soon discovered that to conquer this one region, the richest and most strategic on the island, did not mean the conquest of Ireland. The geographic formations that conditioned the movement of the Irish also prevented the conqueror from moving west. After each invasion, the native Irish gradually reclaimed the ownership of their land.

Christianity existed in Ireland before bandits captured Saint Patrick. In fact, the number of Irish Christians necessitated the appointment of a bishop in 431; yet the church gained its powerful role in Irish life, which it has never lost only when Saint Patrick returned to the island after his escape and his preparation for the life of the missionary on the Continent. The work was not easy, and Saint Patrick faced a considerable number of problems; but his perseverance and that of his disciples soon made the church a thriving force.

The new religion built upon the structure it found in Irish society, and soon the Irish had as much influence upon Christianity -as it had upon them. Naturally, Patrick built his church upon an organization which he had known both in England and on the Continent, that is, upon a government of bishops who ruled territorial dioceses. Before he died a synod had assumed the existence of bishops in fixed sees; but this kind of organization required towns, a certain degree of communication, and a sense of church structure, none of which the Irish possessed. Patrick had also introduced monastic life to Ireland, and within a few years of his death the Irish accepted it as their form of church organization, rather than the European practice of fixed sees, mainly because it suited the impulses of a people grown accustomed to a harsh world in which they looked forward to the next.

The first monastic communities harmonized with the Irish instinct for localism and suspicion of higher authority. In time, bishops became subordinate members of the monastic community, whose task it was to dispense those sacraments without which the community could not survive. Abbots emerged as the church administrators, and their power grew as monks left their monasteries to establish new foundations, all allied to the original institution. This system soon gained sufficient wealth to support numerous scholars and scribes who preserved the manuscripts of the past; simultaneously, it supplied the saints who returned to the Continent to rebuild the church in the wake of the Germanic invasions. Thus, Celtic Ireland that had defied the Romans and had escaped the destruction of the Germanic invasion renounced her isolation for the sake of the church and sent her saints and scholars to the Continent she had once ignored. These missionaries returned to Europe as both Irishmen and Christians. They brought, not the diocesan administration of Rome, but the monastic rule of Ireland; and, therefore, at that early date clearly sketched a pattern—the ability of Ireland to capture those who came to capture her. This theme will constantly reappear in this story.

This golden age of Irish monastic life produced not only the great works of those sons who moved across Europe but also those of the clerics who remained behind. The latter worked at developing the art of illumination during the seventh and eighth centuries. This skill reached its culmination in the famous Book of Kells. This most characteristic work of their art marked the end of Ireland's first golden age. The Book of Kells was never finished because a new threat to Ireland's independence had arrived.[3]

Ireland's geography again influenced her life as she stood squarely on the path of a hardy people who now wanted to explore the world beyond their cold, northern base on the Scandinavian peninsula. In 795 these fearless sailors arrived off the coast of the island of Iona and quickly attacked the Irish monastery there. Repeated visits of the same nature caused the monks to return to Ireland, and for the next forty years the Vikings, or Norsemen, raided Ireland's coasts with regularity. Then in 837 they decided to build a permanent settlement, well fortified, on the banks of the Liffey River where it emptied into the Irish Sea. That settlement eventually became the city of Dublin.[4]

Ireland's political map at the time showed numerous kingdoms and petty overlordships. These groups spent so much time warring among themselves—often with the new arrivals in alliance with one side or another—that they were unable to mount any kind of concerted effort against these foreigners. In this atmosphere of political division at best, and chaos at worst, the Norsemen continued their attacks, founding such towns as Waterford, Limerick, and Cork, but never really penetrating the interior.

As they made these gains on the country's edge, the Irish themselves began to develop greater political cohesion. In theory, they had always possessed a symbol of central government in the form of the high king, but no one holding that title had ever imposed his will upon Ireland's numerous local rulers. Disunity, however, gradually disappeared toward the end of the tenth century, especially with the arrival of Brian Boru as high king in the first decade of the eleventh century. This growth of Irish unity found expression in a movement against the Vikings, and Boru marshaled his forces against the city of Dublin. The resulting Battle of Clontarf in 1014 ended in victory, but at a high price. Boru was killed. His death marked the close of the Norse invasions.

By then the Vikings had accepted Christianity and had become a part of the Irish landscape. In turn, the Irish had accepted many Viking ways. At Clontarf, for instance, both sides used the same weapons and tactics. Furthermore, the Norsemen had built the towns and caused the Irish to look to the sea with all of its possibilities for trade. More importantly, they caused the focus of life to shift from the interior to the Irish sea, where it remained until the peasants arrived in America centuries later. Only then did Ireland's attention turn to the Atlantic and the New World.

At the same time, Boru's establishment of the first effective central authority seriously affected the nation's politics. For most of the early Middle Ages (500-1000) one family controlled the title of high king, but the successful claim of Boru opened the competition to a number of families. For a hundred and fifty years after his death, the title moved from family to family and from region to region. Unfortunately, this destroyed the promise of Boru's era—political stability under an effective central government. The chaos that characterized the years after the Norse invasions in effect paved the way for the arrival of the next would-be conquerors, the Anglo-Normans.

Where the politicians failed in the years before the Anglo-Normans, religious leaders brought reform, unity, and greater power to the Irish. The disruption of the Viking wars created a serious need for religious renewal, but the monastic organization of Ireland's church simply could not supply the changes necessary to meet the spiritual needs of the people. As the clergy realized this, they also encountered the religious reform movement then spreading on the Continent. Bishops and abbots soon demanded changes, and this pressure eventually led to two national synods that replaced the old organization in exchange for the Roman concept of episcopal sees. In 1111 the first synod created twenty-four sees; in 1152 a further change established thirty-six sees, four archbishops, and gave the "pallio" to the archbishops of Armagh, Cashel, Dublin, and Tuam. Strangely enough in the light of this wholesale reform, Pope Adrian IV, the only Englishman ever to sit on the papal throne, gave Henry II, king of England and ruler of vast stretches of France, a commission in 1155 to enter Ireland and set about the task of reforming the church. Why Pope Adrian did this is unclear, but it served as an opening for the English attempt to conquer Ireland.[5]

Henry II could not take advantage of this opportunity in 1155, as he was fully committed to consolidating his power in France. Meanwhile, in Ireland a personal and bitter struggle erupted between two great Irish warrior-kings, Dermot MacMurrough of Lenster and Tiernan O'Rourke. When this ended in MacMurrough's defeat, he left Ireland in search of support with which he could regain his lands. Thus began a process that often recurred in Irish history.

Dermot traveled to England and France to ask Henry II for aid in recovering his lands in Ireland. He found Henry II deep in Aquitaine in 1166, and the shrewd king saw his chance to gain control of Ireland with little direct expense to his own treasury. He gave Dermot a letter in which he asked his subjects to help his newly found Irish ally to regain his rightful position. In spite of the letter, Dermot found little interest in his project among the king's subjects until he got to Wales, where he found Richard FitzGilbert de Clare, the earl of Pembroke (more widely known as "Strongbow"). With the earl's help Dermot gained pledges from many Anglo-Norman lords, and in 1167 he returned to Ireland. For the next hundred years Anglo-Normans arrived. They ravished the country, replaced the native Irish nobility, and generally attempted to subjugate the people. They brought with them the machinery of centralized administration and concepts of town planning. These factors resulted in economic growth, a degree of political stability, and a somewhat Anglicized hierarchy in control of the church.[6]

Yet the Irish did not accept English control and actively sought to reduce their presence. Neither the Anglo-Norman nobles nor the king indicated any willingness to pay the price necessary for full conquest. In effect, the Irish remained in control of much of the country while the English ruled the region around Dublin and the towns. The struggle between them turned in favor of the Irish in the latter half of the thirteenth century. The victories at Callann in 1261 and Athankip in 1270 marked the military turn of fortune, while the Irish attempt to enlist outside aid against the Anglo-Normans marked the beginnings of her many attempts at diplomatic ventures. Her first effort, directed toward Norway, failed; but after the turn of the century Robert Bruce of Scotland decided to take advantage of Irish unrest to defeat the English by way of Ireland. Shortly after his great victory at Bannockburn he crossed the Irish Sea and for a decade disrupted English influence in the island.

These military and diplomatic signs of the Gaelic revival reinforced the cultural advance. As it had so many times in the past, the basic charm of Irish life as well as her customs and traditions began to infiltrate the Anglo-Norman community. Fewer in numbers, the Anglo-Normans married into Irish families, soon acquired the native language, and then rapidly became identified with the old population. The speed and breadth of this assimilation caused the British to enact in 1366 the famous Statutes of the Kilkenny Parliament which proscribed the use of the Irish language, laws, or customs. These acts, directed toward the Anglo-Norman community, which was rapidly becoming the Anglo-Irish community, could not prevent the Gaelic onslaught, as those who came to conquer became more Irish than the Irish themselves. The great de Burgh family of the early years of the Anglo-Norman invasion, for instance, by the later Middle Ages became the Burkes of Connaught and indistinguishable from the old Irish.

As the Gaelic revival reduced English control, militarily and culturally, to the area around Dublin, known as the Pale, the only hope for survival of an Anglo-Norman colony demanded direct English aid. Yet, as the fifteenth century wore on, England's capacity to aid the colony seriously declined. The wars with the Scots in the north and the Hundred Years' War with France taxed England's resources. When this latter struggle ended in 1452, the English entered a period of civil conflict, the famous War of the Roses. In spite of an attempt by Richard II to regain the initiative in Ireland in 1394 (which literally cost him his throne), English influence clearly declined. Then the Anglo-Irish lords became involved in the War of the Roses, and the English government lost effective control of even the Pale. In effect, the events that followed the Battle of Callann in 1261 firmly established a fundamental principle for the future. The Irish used England's troubles at home and abroad to advantage.[7]

II   English Domination

Ireland's native resurgence slowly came to a halt in the years after the War of the Roses. Henry Tudor won control of England in 1485 and took the title of Henry VII. He and his Tudor successors ruled England as absolute monarchs with great success, but they quickly saw the need to follow a defensive policy with respect to Ireland. To rule England the Tudors needed a quiet and friendly Ireland, and this time they would pay the price.

Henry VII started by regaining control of the area around Dublin and what machinery of government had remained after the disruptions of civil war. In 1494 he sent Sir Edward Poynings with instructions to reduce the country to "whole and perfect obedience." Once there, Poynings called for a Parliament to meet in December, 1494. This legislative body made history. It decreed that the frontier of the Pale should be defended; constables should be of English birth; Irish customs and dress be proscribed; and, finally, that the Irish Parliament would meet only after royal permission had been granted and after the king and Council had approved measures to be enacted. Henry VII had only one purpose in mind when he forced these laws upon what remained of the old English colony—to prevent any possibility of a pretender using the Pale as a base of attack on his throne. Only later did these laws take on a different meaning, but as long as a loyal subject ruled the English portion of Ireland, Henry VII remained outside Irish affairs. He made no attempt to enlarge the area under English domination.

Henry VIII, who became king in 1509, followed his father's Irish policy for ten years, mainly because it was cheaper to have

Anglo-Irish nobles rule in Ireland than to attempt the suppression of the country. Then in 1519 he decided he needed greater control over the island. He removed the earl of Kildare from his post in Ireland and made the Great Earl of Surrey his representative with orders to reduce Ireland to his will. Surrey failed to gain any effective control over the Anglo-Irish lords and within two years he asked for a large force to accomplish his mission. Henry, however, did not want to pay that high a price; Surrey returned to England, and Henry returned the earl of Kildare to his old position. Ireland had avoided more effective English domination.

The affair marked the start of a new unity in Irish life. The native Irish and those Anglo-Normans who had accepted Gaelic traditions had opposed Henry's effort to reduce their independence for obvious reasons, but the Anglo-Normans in the Pale also opposed him. Then when Henry broke with Rome and the English Parliament declared him to be the Supreme Head of the Church in England, these elements quickly found another cause for joint action. Henry again called the earl of Kildare to London, but the earl's son, Thomas, remained in control of the English colony. When a rumor reached Ireland that his father had been executed, Thomas revolted against the king and gained some support because of Henry's religious policies.

At this point, Henry decided that Ireland had to be conquered, if for no other reason than to remove any possibility of the opposition using Ireland as a base against him. Like many Englishmen, Henry also suffered from dreams of imperialism and saw in Ireland England's first experiment in colonization. Henry sent William Skiffington to Ireland with a large force. The English army immediately surrounded "Silken" Thomas' stronghold at Maynooth and destroyed the walls with artillery. Skiffington then ordered the execution of the survivors. "The pardon of Maynooth" was another of a long series of unfortunate acts that created that senseless bitterness that has characterized Anglo-Irish affairs for centuries and continues in the current crises in Northern Ireland. Once in control of the Pale, Henry introduced the Reformation and did to Ireland what he was doing to England. Religious houses were dissolved, church lands were confiscated, and numerous other acts were passed which culminated in Ireland's Parliament declaring Henry the Supreme Head of the Church in Ireland.[8]

The conquest of the Irish Pale, however, did not mean the

conquest of old Ireland; nor did Henry's Reformation extend beyond the Pale and the towns. For the rest of Ireland, Henry decided to negotiate with the Irish lords and those English rebels who had accepted the Gaelic tradition, all of whom virtually ruled as independent kings. He could not afford a full-scale conquest and settled for pledges of allegiance, which he received with little opposition, as most of Ireland's lords realized they meant nothing.

Political allegiance, however, did not include religious conformity. In old Ireland, the priests rallied both the native Irish and the Gaelicized English rebels to the Roman church, while many Englishmen in areas of Henry's control also supported the old religion. Henry's religious decisions had created a situation that would eventually unite the three basic components of Irish life in opposition to the king and England. Soon Henry's church, and Elizabeth's that followed, became the religion of the new English colony and of the official class. What was once a purely political question, tinged with conflicting national ties, now became a religious question as well.

Henry's successors continued his basic policy of gaining control of Ireland through negotiation rather than force, but under Elizabeth the policy eventually failed. She had some success with Henry's approach, but by the 1590's she found herself faced with the decision to use force. She first moved against Munster where she found considerable opposition, but once her forces suppressed the Irish rebels in Munster, she had less trouble with Connaught. When she moved against Ulster, she encountered the strongest opposition under the leadership of Hugh O'Neill, earl of Tyrone. The struggle ended in 1603, the year of Elizabeth's death.

Elizabeth's Irish policy had far-reaching implications. The defeat of O'Neill at Kinsale in 1603 eventually led to the self-imposed exile of O'Neill and of ninety of his followers. This left Ulster leaderless, and Elizabeth's successor, James I, was free to implement his policy with singular abandon. Elizabeth had only experimented in the areas of Munster and Connaught with the concept of establishing plantations; that is, of taking land from the disloyal, whether Irish or Anglo-Irish, and giving it to loyal subjects transported to Ireland for that specific reason. Under James I Ulster was to be colonized. The Scots and English arrived to build towns, work the soil, create markets, and build industries. Unfortunately, for the future, no matter how hard the Protestant loyalists worked to fill the province, pockets of Catholics remained, embittered, degraded, and anxious for an opportunity to strike back.[9]

The issue, now clearly one of religion, caused a response from Rome. Now in the midst of her own Counter-Reformation, Rome strengthened the administration of the Irish church, established schools on the Continent for the training of Irish priests, and intensified her efforts to remain in contact with the people. Under that kind of activity and in spite of royal policy, Catholicism thrived.

Meanwhile, the Anglo-Normans who had remained Catholic felt seriously threatened. They wanted to preserve their political position while practicing their religion, and they sought legal guarantees from the king. In 1628 Charles I acknowledged certain rights of these lords in exchange for payment. He did the same thing in England, but in 1629 he revoked the English "Petition of Rights" and shortly thereafter renounced his earlier statement in support of Anglo-Norman privileges in Ireland. He sent Sir Thomas Wentworth to establish a strong government, and this new representative of the King soon used the Irish Parliament for his own purposes. The practice of land confiscation continued, regardless of who owned it—old Irish, Gaelicized Normans or Anglo-Norman Catholics. The only issue which determined who would own the land was loyalty. Yet in 1640 Charles faced civil war. This gave the Anglo-Normans the chance to regain their rights—by negotiating a new agreement with Charles I. Unfortunately, they dealt with and supported the wrong side. When Charles I lost the war, the Catholics in Ireland faced Protestant England.

Cromwell became the military dictator of England after the death of Charles, but he soon encountered the same basic problem that his royal predecessors had faced. He had to suppress Ireland to deny its use as a base for an attack upon his position by his enemies. He arrived with an army in 1649, laid siege to the town of Drogheda, captured it, and slaughtered the entire population. The fate of that town and the ruthlessness of Cromwell's methods placed an indelible mark upon the Irish, but he succeeded in destroying open and effective opposition. Once he had done that, he completely reworked the land structure. Land owned by those in rebellion became the property of Cromwell's government, which then distributed its holdings to those who had made the victory possible. What Elizabeth had started on a small scale and James I applied to Ulster with such abandon, Cromwell applied to the rest of the country. The struggle between Ireland and England now became economic as well as political and religious. The successive attempts at a solution of the Irish problem from Henry VII to Cromwell only complicated the relations between the two nations and enlarged the possibility for bitter reprisals from both sides.[10]

Cromwell died in 1658, and his death led to the restoration of the monarchy two years later. The arrival of Charles II raised the hope of the Catholic landlords that they would regain their lands, and a few did receive control of areas that had been confiscated. However, the Cromwellian land settlement for the most part remained. Charles II permitted Catholics to practice their religion with little inconvenience, but they felt their second-class status and simply waited for the opportunity to regain their former positions. Ireland now had only two groups, Catholics and transplanted Protestants.

The country remained relatively quiet until James II followed his brother to the throne in 1685. The new king had married a French princess in his youth and came to the throne an announced Catholic. Catholics in Ireland immediately felt he would respond to their needs. At first James II seemed more interested in maintaining the English position in Ireland with his endorsement of the land settlement and the Protestant church, the very pillars of English rule in Ireland. Soon, however, he replaced his Protestant brother-in-law, Lord Clarendon, as the lord lieutenant of Ireland with the Catholic Richard Talbot, the earl of Tryconnell. The new viceroy began to appoint Catholics to various government offices and to the army. Plans were laid for a new Parliament which would have a Catholic majority, but all these hopes crumbled with the Glorious Revolution in England.

In 1688 William of Orange, the husband of James II's Protestant-daughter, Mary, landed in England at the request of Parliament. The move forced James to flee to France; but his viceroy held Ireland for him, and in March, 1689 he landed at Kinsale with French troops. Yet James failed to subdue the Protestant North, which opened the way for William to land in Ireland. The two kings met in July, 1690, at the Battle of the Boyne. James and the Catholic cause lost, Dublin fell to William, and the Catholics had to retreat across the Shannon. The defeat at Aughrim followed, and the Protestants now had the power to destroy any force Catholics could bring to the field. William, however, desired an end to this conflict in order to concentrate his effort on the continental struggle against Louis XIV of France. Consequently, he signed the Treaty of Limerick on October 3, 1691. Catholics received religious toleration, security of their property, and the right to leave Ireland for Europe if they so desired. As a result of the latter provision, fourteen thousand Irish troops under Patrick Sarsfield left for France, and the legend of the "wild Geese" was born. Those that remained soon discovered that the Protestant minority would not honor the terms of the treaty, and Catholics got less than they had anticipated. Yet the disagreement over the Treaty of Limerick and what it meant soon lost significance in the aftermath that followed.[11]

The significant events of eighteenth-century Irish history began with Limerick and ended in 1778 with the first attempt to give Catholics some voice in the affairs of the island. In those eighty-seven years the Protestant majority erected by legislation an economic and social structure that almost denied Catholics the right to exist. Penal laws were passed with the sole aim of keeping Catholics in a permanent state of subjection. The worse part of this period extended from 1691 to 1716 during which time the possibility of Ireland's being used as a base against the king was strongest. After 1716 those aspects of the laws which sought the end of Catholicism lapsed, and the church was able to provide enough priests and bishops to survive and reform itself somewhat. On the political side, however, the prescribing of an oath which no Catholic could take virtually eliminated them from government and this continued until 1778. On the economic side, Catholic-controlled land dropped from 14 percent in 1691 to less than 5 percent in 1778. In the period from Elizabeth to 1778 the English government literally drove Catholics from the landowning class. The Catholic upper and middle classes ceased to exist, the result of a deliberate policy of minority oppression of the majority.

In addition to the remnants of an embittered upper class which these policies created, London authorities faced the problem of a Catholic peasant class whose standard of living continued to decline throughout the eighteenth century. A rising population and short-term land leases led to higher rents. Numerous restrictions on trade and manufacturing forced rents higher as the population had no outlet other than to turn to agriculture. In short, both upper- and lower-class Catholics had serious grievances against the government; but they could do little until world conflicts weakened

England's position and Protestant leaders discovered that they too had reason to complain.[12]

III *Nationalism*

The great attempt to free Ireland from English domination that occurred in the last quarter of the eighteenth century started as a movement among Catholics. The penal laws rested to an extent upon a belief that Catholics were disloyal. Catholic spokesmen from the largely nonexistent middle class and the few remnants of the old aristocracy argued that Catholics were not disloyal and offered as proof their response in the Seven Years' War when Protestant England fought Catholic France. In that conflict Catholics did in fact remain loyal to England, and the British government decided to make every effort to placate the people in case the French attempted an invasion of Ireland. In 1762 London prepared plans to arm Catholics and bring them into the British army for use in Portugal. At the same time, certain members of Parliament wanted to introduce a bill which would permit Catholics to take mortgages on land. Yet both of these measures simply aroused the Protestants in Ireland, who saw them as attempts to destroy their position in Irish life. The conservatives had an unwilling ally in the agrarian disorders that appeared at this time, especially in Munster and Ulster. Secret societies of Whiteboys directed their violent attacks against rack-rents, tithes, unemployment, and other problems. The government responded with a policy of coercion which in effect admitted that Ireland was in a state of war. The attempt to bring Catholics into the government thus failed both because of the extreme fears of Protestants and because of the extreme reaction of Catholics. The middle- and upper-class Catholics wanted a peaceful end to penal laws and coercion; but the peasants had learned to defy established authority, and the Gaelic poets of that age kept the fire of defiance alive.

However, the whole Irish political pattern radically changed with the coming of the American Revolution.[13] Once again England was at war with France; and the national interest again demanded some form of Irish relief bill if the government wanted the Irish to remain loyal and supply the hoped-for necessary recruits to fill the ranks of the British army. In 1778, therefore, the government introduced and pushed through the Irish Parliament a bill that permitted

Catholics to take long term leases on land. The real start to full emancipation had begun.

While the American Revolution influenced Catholics, it also stirred the Protestant Anglo-Irish ascendancy. First, the Protestants felt that the war left the island open to a French invasion and responded by forming militia units which they called the "Volunteers." This military response changed when the volunteer units became political debating clubs. Coupled with the American movement toward independence, these events forged the Irish Protestants into a political force that demanded free trade and the end to England's restrictions upon Ireland's economy. The British surrendered to these demands in 1779, but the concession came too late. Under the leadership of Henry Grattan rising Irish Protestant nationalism demanded an end to the subordination of the Irish Parliament to England, and again the British agreed. Soon all that remained of the old powers was the king's right to veto bills.[14]

These changes created a situation where Ireland had become in theory an independent state under a king who also ruled England. In reality, however, Ireland's executive remained subject to the government in London whose leaders had great power over the Irish Parliament because of various legal and illegal means of gaining a majority on any given issue. In this situation some voices called for the reform of Parliament to make it more responsive to the Irish people. Here Catholic and Protestant political leadership joined forces. Henry Flood first suggested such a policy as early as 1783, but to no avail, since few people felt any pressing need for change. For the next six years this demand for reform lay dormant, but in 1789 the French Revolution charged the atmosphere in both Ireland and England. Henry Grattan now took up the cry for reform, but he was interested only in reducing the London government's control over the Irish Parliament. By 1789 the whole movement for parliamentary reform had stimulated the demand for Catholic emancipation. Theobald Wolfe Tone saw this new development and called for both emancipation and reform as the only program that would solve the nation's needs. Tone then combined forces with the Belfast Society of United Irishmen and later with the Dublin Society of United Irishmen, then under the leadership of Napper Tandy.

While these radical elements demanded complete emancipation, moderate Catholics gained at least a degree of success in their battle against the Penal Code. Under the leadership of John Keogh, a Catholic Committee appeared in Dublin. To demonstrate that this body spoke for the Catholics of the nation, Keogh called a convention to meet in December, 1792. The success of this meeting led to a call for a repeal of the Penal Codes and in 1793 the government, again fearful of a French invasion, pushed a relief bill through Parliament that removed all disabilities except that of holding office, including seats in Parliament. It also gave Catholics the right to vote, which would have important future ramifications.

The success of this moderate Catholic movement did not stem the tide of rising agrarian crime. The population continued to grow. Competition for land increased and violence followed. The higher and higher rents and tithes continued to reduce the standard of living. The peasants' only recourse was violence, as no government official paid any attention to their problems. Full-scale revolts occurred in Ulster. These in turn led to the formation of the Orange Society, a Protestant protective association.

In the face of this violence, the radical United Irishmen formed a new program calling for emancipation, parliamentary reform, and independence. In 1796 Tone urged the French government to take advantage of Irish unrest, and the French, as usual, saw an opportunity to strike at England. They decided to take the risk. Fourteen thousand troops set sail for Ireland, but because of numerous weather problems and other factors, they never landed. Yet the United Irishmen did not halt their own plans, and in 1798 a revolt occurred. The English quickly defeated the Irish forces at Vinegar Hill before the arrival of a second French expedition and the whole episode ended in failure.

However, the men who led that revolution did influence the thoughts of British Prime Minister William Pitt, who decided to solve the crises of Ireland. His solution was simple: unite the two Parliaments. Henry Grattan, the Protestant leader, exploded and successfully led the fight against the plan in the Irish Parliament, where it was defeated in 1799 by five votes. Then the real relationship between the two countries clearly emerged. Pitt used his many powers to influence Irish legislators, and in 1800 the Irish Parliament voted to dissolve itself. On January 1, 1801, Ireland became an integral part of the United Kingdom. Protestant Irish members would sit in the English Parliament. Pitt could now keep his eyes on Ireland and control her directly.[15]

Not everyone appreciated the union, however, and almost as an anticlimax Robert Emmet, an Irish Catholic, led the remnants of the United Irishmen in revolt in 1803. Hopeless from the start, the attempt failed, and Robert Emmet was executed. Yet before he died he delivered his speech upon the dock which inspired Irishmen to follow his lead for the next hundred and twenty years.

The union began with a great degree of promise since Pitt had agreed that Catholic emancipation would follow. The king, however, opposed such a move as did the majority of Pitt's cabinet. As a result, for the next thirty years Irish and English statesmen literally ignored the one great pressing problem—land—and concentrated upon the struggle for emancipation, the story of which is really the story of Daniel O'Connell. [16]

Born in 1775, O'Connell qualified as a lawyer in 1798 and soon became one of the nation's most successful barristers, but in 1813 he decided to devote more time to politics. In that same year the government in London made a tragic mistake by attempting to influence the selection of Catholic bishops for Irish sees. The blunder literally politicized the church and the clergy, and for ten years O'Connell watched that process. In 1823, when he formed the Catholic Association, which was devoted to full emancipation, he enlisted the local clergy as his organizers at the grass-roots level. In addition, he struck upon the ingenious device of establishing a penny-a-month rent, "The Catholic rent," which everyone could pay.

The combination led to the first real mass political movement in Irish history, and in the general elections of 1826 O'Connell proved that his cadres would defeat any candidate who opposed emancipation. Catholics still had to vote for Protestants because they could not sit in Parliament, but O'Connell hoped that his association would make such a successful showing at the next general election the English would have to concede. O'Connell never had the opportunity to implement this plan, for in 1828 Vesey Fitzgerald, a Protestant member of Parliament from Clare, accepted a post in the cabinet and had to stand for reelection. O'Connell knew he had to order the association to oppose the popular Fitzgerald and spent some time trying to find a Protestant who would run against him on an emancipation platform. But none would come forward. Then in an absolutely brilliant stroke, O'Connell decided to run himself. As a Catholic, of course, he could not sit in Parliament if he won, but no law said he could not run.

The association then swung into high gear as the priests organized their flocks in support of O'Connell. When the results were known, the priests had marched their parishioners to a 2,057 to 982 victory for the cause. Their effort broke the back of English opposition, and on April 13, 1829 Parliament passed a bill that granted Catholic emancipation. O'Connell had won; he was the first Catholic to sit in Parliament from an Irish seat in many years. Others followed quickly.

For the next twelve years O'Connell led a small band of fellow Catholics in Parliament who supported the Liberal party and in this way gained a number of concessions for Ireland. Then in 1841, the Conservatives returned to power, and O'Connell's power position in Parliament disappeared. At age sixty-six O'Connell decided to fight for the repeal of the Act of Union. He immediately formed the Repeal Association, organized it along lines similar to the Catholic Association, and added the technique of the "monster meeting," which attracted hundreds of thousands of peasants. In 1843, at the height of the agitation, O'Connell held forty of these meetings as he marshaled the forces of Ireland on the side of repeal. However, the prime minister of England, William Peel, was not moved, nor did anyone in Parliament come to O'Connell's aid. In fact, Englishmen saw the demand for repeal as an effort to destroy the empire, and Peel vowed he would not permit this. When O'Connell announced plans for a grand monster meeting at Clontarf for October 8, 1843, the authorities decided to move. They banned the meeting on the assumption that O'Connell, now the leader of Ireland and fundamentally a nonviolent person, would not resort to force. They were right, and O'Connell's decision marked the end of his Repeal Association. Money continued to arrive. In fact, in 1844 it totaled more than in 1843, and O'Connell did not die until 1847. However, the strength of the movement had been broken, and O'Connell's methods proved incapable of gaining what Ireland wanted. The collapse of O'Connell gave the thrust of events to another group of men, known as the "Young Irelanders," but they and the whole world of politics soon fell victim to the Great Famine. These two developments changed the whole course of Irish history as they combined to create another Irish nation, this time across the sea in America. [17]

CHAPTER 2

Irish-America Before the "Great Migration"

I Colonial Years

THE America to which the Irish traveled in the late 1840's was neither young nor old; nor were the Irish new to her or America to them. In fact, Americans and Irishmen had one important relationship in common—England.

Most American histories start with the arrival of the Indians after the long journey from Asia, with travels of Leif Ericson, or with the discoveries of Columbus, yet the America that existed in the 1840's began only with the arrival of English settlers in 1607. Their social, political, economic, and religious ideals, concepts, and institutions, which grew out of England's medieval experience, laid the foundations of the America the famine Irish found two hundred and forty years later. The understanding of that America demands an understanding of those values.

A number of cultural influences (Celtic, Roman, German, Dane, Norse, and Norman), all squeezed into a relatively small waterlocked area, produced the England that William I conquered in 1066. Although he operated a relatively effective government, those who followed up to 1485 failed to produce a central authority with sufficient power to impose its will upon the tendency toward localism which those varied cultural influences sustained. In that situation, the people developed political ideals and institutions which by 1485 Englishmen accepted without question.

The king did not live above the law or beyond the rights of his people. Englishmen had rights of self-government as well as representative government. They believed that the state had the obligation to provide a world in which man could develop unhampered by government edict. Even under the absolute rule of the Tudors, which followed the end of civil war in 1485, neither the ruled nor the rulers could ignore such ideas. Although very much controlled by those monarchs, Parliament continued to sit, and the concept of representation did not disappear. On the eve of the founding of Jamestown, the English nation, including those who arrived off the coast of North America in 1607, held true to those beliefs in their rights as Englishmen that their medieval experience had created.[1]

Shortly after the founding of Jamestown, these Englishmen exercised their rights and forced the town's government to become more responsive to the needs of the people. The London Company in its charter from the Crown received the right to determine the colony's form of government. In typical corporate fashion, they established a committee to rule Jamestown, but that experiment failed to solve the colony's problems. Within a year the discontent created an antigovernment party under the leadership of John Smith. This movement in effect changed the fundamental structure of government from a committee executive to rule by one man with the advice of a council. Ten years later the London Company approved the establishment of a representative legislative body. Within twelve years of its founding, Virginia had a form of government similar to that of England. The colonies that followed, regardless of how they started, soon acquired similar forms, characterized by self-government, representative government, responsiveness to the needs of the people, and participation by a class of people that would have been excluded from politics if they had remained in England.[2] In short, political mobility for both groups and individuals existed in America from the start. Economic and social mobility followed, in direct contrast to what was happening in Ireland in particular and in Europe in general. By the end of the seventeenth century this reputation for an open society with opportunity for all began to convince many people to move to America.

This awareness of the blessings to be found in the colonies soon linked Ireland to America. The Glorious Revolution of 1689 ended with Parliament in control of England and, after the Treaty of Limerick, in control of Ireland. Unfortunately for everyone in Ireland, Catholic and Protestant alike, those who ruled Parliament saw Ireland through the eyes of the mercantilists. In their minds, London could permit no Irishman, Catholic or Protestant, to compete with the businessmen of England. As a result, Ireland's Catholics suffered under the famous Penal Codes while Protestants in the North suffered from harsh economic restrictions. Coupled to their Presbyterian dislike of the established Anglican church and the high rents they had to pay to absentee landlords, these relatively new Irishmen began to look for greener pastures. Fully aware of events and trends in the American colonies, they soon began to leave Ireland for America. The first mass exodus came in 1717-18, the result of insecure land tenure arrangements, and in the late 1720's a second, heavier wave of emigration developed. The movement continued over the years until on the eve of the American Revolution a quarter of a million Irish immigrants had arrived.[3]

These hardy people, who possessed qualities that made them fierce defenders of their homes, at first moved into New England where they established Londonderry in New Hampshire and Worcester in Massachusetts. Later they found Pennsylvania's greater economic opportunities and religious freedom more conducive to their needs. Many traveled through Virginia into the back country of the Carolinas. Philadelphia then became the main port for their debarkation; but after a number of immigrant ships made the run directly to Charleston in the mid-1730's, large numbers entered the colonies at that point. In both places, the majority rushed to the frontier where, threatened only by Indians, they could build their own world free from outside influence.[4]

Few Irish Catholics, mostly servants, arrived during this period, and those who did settled for the most part in Pennsylvania and Maryland. Some came with wealth, and many established prosperous lives as merchants and landowners, but no mass movement developed in southern Ireland. The Protestant colonies in America simply did not want that kind of immigrant.

Meanwhile, other groups came to America (large numbers of discontented Germans with their various shades of Protestantism, a relatively small number of French Huguenots, some Scots from Scotland, and a scattering of Jews). All contributed to America's rapidly growing population (300,000 in 1690 to 1,600,000 in 1760) and added significantly to its complexity.[5] More important, they profoundly affected America's politics and thus paved the road for the Irish to make their contribution to American life.

These new immigrants came in the midst of fundamental political change in America. Where prior to 1688 power tended to reside in the governor's house or the council, after 1688 the lower, popularly elected houses in the colonies rapidly increased their power by gaining control of the purse and the distribution of patronage. By 1754 London recognized that the New York Assembly literally controlled all offices of the colonial government, and by 1763 no one disputed the power of the various assemblies to rule their own destinies.

Relatively few, however, recognized the effect this shift of power had upon America's politics. As popularly elected bodies, the assemblies were open to the pressures generated by the complexity that America's population, economic interests, and social composition generated. By the time of the accession of George III, faction politics existed as fully in America as in England, and the politician's role centered in his ability to compromise such differences into accepted policy. This proved difficult because alliances between the various factions, never permanent, existed only for the duration of a specific issue. Furthermore, effective politics stopped at the states' borders, as those factions with similar interests in the various colonies saw no necessity to unite. What happened in Pennsylvania had no powerful claim upon the thoughts of a New Yorker or a Virginian. Not until the events that occurred between 1763 and 1775 did America's politicians realize that their interests crossed boundaries. That realization eventually resulted in the Declaration of Independence. America became a nation, as political factions from New England to Georgia formed against the loyalist minority. In that atmosphere, the nation embarked upon a war of revolution.[6]

II   *Revolution and Political Change*

Unity on the major issue, however, did not end faction politics. Even as the war approached, many refused to follow the lead of radicals and moderates, yet they did not organize effectively at the national level. Those who favored England in the dispute had no effective counterpart to the Committee of Correspondence which united those in the various colonies who opposed English policies. Furthermore, the majority, although unified in opposing England, disagreed on most of the other questions of the day, including how to counter English threats to colonial freedom. In the course of the Revolutionary War, control of events tended to flow from one faction to the other, with the more radical elements dominating at the start, and the more conservative ones at the end, of the war.

These twin developments—the unification of interests and continued divisions—engulfed the immigrants from Ireland who by

1763 had already appeared as one of many political factions. Scotch-Irish from New England to South Carolina supported the revolution, but many remained loyal to the Crown. In New England those on the frontier fought in the campaigns against Burgoyne in 1777; but, when the British occupied Boston in 1775, a loyal militia unit was formed under the title of Loyal Irish Volunteers. The Scotch-Irish in Pennsylvania fought hard for the revolution, but did so no less to destroy the proprietary government of Pennsylvania as to eliminate English control of the colonies. Pennsylvania's established political power had long ignored the legitimate demands of the frontiersmen whose frustration had erupted in a violent display when the Paxton Boys marched on Philadelphia in 1764. Yet in Philadelphia the British recruited a loyal regiment, Volunteers of Ireland, comprising both Irish-Catholics and many Scotch-Irish dissenters from the Continental Army. In North and South Carolina the reverse was true, where for the most part the Scotch-Irish on the frontier remained loyal, mainly because of bitter memories of the Regulator movement of the 1760's. The eastern powers that had denied legitimate demands of the frontier now led the revolution and wanted the Scotch-Irish to fight at their side. The numerous appeals fell on deaf ears, however.[7] Thus, although this particular faction from Ireland in one sense united at the national level, disagreements on fundamental policy continued to exist.

Such disagreements, among and within the various elements in the political world, clearly foreshadowed the nature of American politics which emerged in the constitutional controversies that followed the ratification of the Articles of Confederation and the arrival of peace in 1783. The articles theoretically provided the political machinery at the national level, while the Paris Peace Treaty removed the only issue upon which the factions in the various states could agree. Consequently, factional politics reappeared at the state level and in Congress as well. Unfortunately, the weakness of the national machinery permitted factions to operate in Congress without restraint, and government failed to function. This led to the writing of a new constitution that would give the national government sufficient power, but the discussions at the Constitutional Convention that convened in Philadelphia in 1787 failed to solve a fundamental need. The Constitution it produced formalized and placed on a permanent basis what had existed on the surface of American life since 1763—national unity—but it did not provide the basis for the creation of a more permanent union of those similar interests or factions that existed within the states. Congress existed and the various states could send their representatives to that body, but no permanent machinery existed around which those with similar interests from the various states could unite. Until that appeared, immigrant groups like the Irish had little hope of influencing national politics.

Alexander Hamilton, essentially a party man, crystallized the issue for all to see: first, when he, along with others, issued the Federalist Papers; second, when he issued his famous reports on public credit and manufactures. In effect, these papers proposed a principle of government, a political philosophy which appealed to certain factions in all states, and these Americans gravitated toward the then emerging Federalist party. Those opposed to his idea of government sought a home of their own. In this way, Hamilton brought certain factions that existed at the state level into a semipermanent unity. They retained their factional interests both on the local and national scene, but now they lived within an extralegal structure, the political party.

Those who opposed Hamilton's views had to find a place of their own, and they gravitated toward the leadership of Thomas Jefferson. The father of American liberalism reacted to the Hamiltonian success, literally and quite reluctantly, by groping along the trail to a political party of his own. The election of 1796 pushed him further down that road, and the Alien and Sedition Acts only confirmed the rightness of that decision. The work of organization then began in earnest, and Jefferson now had a political party that united similar factions in the various states in time for the campaign of 1800. His success in that election proved the need for the party structure. The revolutionary and constitutional decades raised America's faction politics to the national level and created the need for national political organizations in which the Irish eventually could find room to maneuver.[8]

Meanwhile, in the 1780's immigration from Ulster revived, and the British became alarmed at its steady rate. In 1788 the Irish government banned the emigration of skilled artisans, and in 1803 Parliament passed the Passenger Act, which reduced the number of emigrants a ship could carry. In spite of such laws, however, the Irish continued to emigrate. In the 1790's they came from the South as well as the North. Many who came were artisans and more often than not possessed means and education. At the same time, the activities of the United Irishmen in the early 1790's forced the British government to drive radical leaders from Ireland. James Reynolds, Wolfe Tone, Hamilton Rowan, and even Napper Tandy arrived in the United States by 1795. They mingled with the Irish in New York and Philadelphia, many of whom, like Mathew Carey, a bookseller and printer, had already risen to a position of responsibility. The failure of the 1798 revolution in Ireland forced more revolutionary leaders to settle in various parts of America. One, for instance, eventually settled in Petersburg, Virginia, where he remained a prominent voice in the town's life for fifty years. Many, like Tone, remained for only a short time and were exiles rather than immigrants, while others, like Reynolds, stayed to lead the growing ranks of Irish-Americans, lumped into sharply defined communities in Philadelphia and New York.[9] Possibly they recognized the kind of political life that was emerging in America and realized the opportunities it afforded.

The very appearance of Irishmen under adequate leadership, among other things, prompted the Federalist party to oppose the importation of "wild" foreigners. President John Adams led his administration in accepting the Alien and Sedition Acts, only to infuriate the Irish. Jefferson fought these acts on principle, but one should not doubt his interest in attracting a particular class of voters to his cause. Already by 1800 the Irish in large numbers lived in Philadelphia and New York; some claimed, not without a degree of validity, that Jefferson carried New York because he won the affection of Irish voters. Not only had Jefferson and the Irish recognized the political facts of life, but two years after the election even Hamilton indicated an interest in gaining immigrant votes.[10]

Jefferson entered office on March 4, 1801, with a classic statement of the liberal philosophy, but his deeds did not match his words. All too soon he learned that he could not reverse the policies of the previous administration. He even came to appreciate Hamilton's principles. By the end of his second administration Jefferson and his party had, in effect, merged the two traditions; and, although disagreement continued on many specific questions, the majority of Americans agreed. A consensus on fundamental principles, so essential for American politics, had arrived on the national scene. Not until the congressional elections of 1810 did any sign of a breakdown of that consensus appear. By then, however, events rapidly led the nation into the War of 1812. Yet the sharp divisions in the population which the war generated only masked the basic consensus; they did not destroy it.

In effect, the events from the Revolutionary War to the War of 1812 brought that essential nature of American life, best described by the word *pluralism*, to the national level. America was now a very complex society with wide differences in population, economic enterprise, and political life, but all of these elements accepted a basic sense of unity. When the war ended, unity, not disunity, gained the ascendancy.

The Irish played no major role in American life during the years of Jefferson's and Madison's administrations, except in isolated instances on the local level. They did continue to emigrate; but, as the Napoleonic Wars intensified and England needed more and more sailors, London authorized the boarding of immigrant ships from Ireland on the high seas to impress their load of British citizens into naval service. The Irish in America, now capable of supporting their own press, bitterly denounced these acts which, tied to their Irish nationalism, explains why they so enthusiastically endorsed the War of 1812. By 1810 these acts slowed immigrant traffic considerably. With the outbreak of war two years later, the movement stopped completely.[11]

Thanks to Andrew Jackson's victory at New Orleans after the peace treaty had been signed, the War of 1812 ended in a great outpouring of national unity, and for eight years Americans experienced what one historian has called the "Era of Good Feelings." Political factions, at least on the national level, played down their differences, and real opposition simply did not exist as the political descendants of Jefferson publicly and privately accepted the ideals and policies of Hamilton. Henry Clay, John C. Calhoun, James Monroe, and others accepted the tariff and the need for a second national bank., Yet under this atmosphere of unity and calm, changes occurred that would have a profound influence on Americans in general and on the Irish in particular.

III   *New Politics in America*

From 1800 to 1824 Americans tended to move westward. The magnitude of this migration created six new states before 1819, and for the first time frontier elements made their voices heard at the national level through spokesmen completely dependent upon them. The western interest, quite different from that of the original established coastal regions, had appeared. It added to the complexity of America—and in the search for consensus and policies acceptable to the nation as a whole—greatly increased the demands upon statesmanship and party discipline.

In addition to the westward movement, other significant economic changes occurred, especially those resulting from industrialization. As early as 1815, the machine started to display its power in the South. A simple device, the cotton gin, increased the longevity of slavery as an institution by increasing the capacity of the South to produce cotton. Together with the application of machines to the textile industry, which further increased the demand for cotton, this simple device made that fiber "king" in that part of America. In the North, industrialization led mainly to a considerable increase in the number and volume of manufactured products. Factories appeared, towns and cities grew, and the phenomenon of the urban dweller with all of his problems began to displace the rural American as typical. Production capacity and population figures increased rapidly as America learned to support a large urban labor force.

In this kind of world the Irish immigrant who came after 1815 found great opportunity. But as time passed such opportunities became increasingly limited to the lowest stratum of the economic scale. The males worked on the canals and then on the railroads that feasted upon the westward movement. As they went West, they formed Irish enclaves across America. Their female counterparts became the servant girls of America's wealthy. Together they created the growing numbers of Irish born in America. At the same time they kept the flame of nationalism alive by reading the larger and larger columns of the Irish-American press. The *Truth Teller* appeared in New York in 1825. The Boston *Pilot* appeared thirteen years later. The work of O'Connell's emancipation movement during the 1820's also fueled the fire of nationalism, and the Irish in America responded with money and words of encouragement to his Catholic Association.

For the most part, the Irish remained in the cities along the eastern seaboard and in New England, New York, Pennsylvania, and New Jersey. Their heavy concentrations gave them significant political power on the local level and at times on the state and national level. It also enabled them to take advantage of the changes that the western movement and the economic development brought to these old, established cities and states.[12]

These developments, especially after the War of 1812, tended to create in the American mind a sense of openness, opportunity, and optimism. People began to argue; if opportunity existed in both land and economics, it should also exist in politics. Such ideas were influential in changing the political structure. The constitutions of the new states had already given the people greater and more direct voice in the selection of political leadership, and soon new constitutions in the old states eliminated restrictions on the right to vote. Ballots replaced *viva voce* voting. Politicians reorganized their election campaign strategies. Where before they had to deal with only a handful of legislators who always won reelection, now they had to appeal to the masses. The orator entered politics and communicated with large numbers of voters at monster rallies.[13] Newspapers multiplied as the political editor became essential to any campaign.

Gradually, these changes appeared at the local, then the state, and finally at the national level during and after the election of 1824. In that campaign no candidate won the necessary number of electoral votes; consequently, the politicians in the House of Representatives gave the White House to John Quincy Adams in what many saw as a flagrant disregard of the people's preference for the more popular hero, Andrew Jackson. Jackson, the product of a Scotch-Irish family and now the symbol of the common man, claimed backroom political manipulators had cheated the will of the people when they gave Adams the White House.

For four years Jackson's followers relentlessly worked to forge a combination of interests and factions in all sections into a new national political party. By 1828, they had constructed a solid phalanx of followers in Congress, subsidized a chain of newspapers, essential for any campaign, and organized the party in every state. John C. Calhoun led the South behind Jackson, and Thomas H. Benton added the West. Combined with New York and Virginia, these blocs gave Jackson the power to win. To each of these sections and to each interest within each section he spoke the words they wished to hear. With this organization as a base, in 1828 Jackson polled 59 percent of the popular vote, took the South and the West, and added Pennsylvania and most of New York.

The new politics had arrived. The role of the politician remained the same—to forge the many interests in the nation into a majority—but now the whole focus centered upon the machine as the only tool with which the political boss could fulfill his role. Party organization on a permanent basis became essential. Jackson left his mark.[14] He had learned how to conquer the growing pluralism in American life and to control the machinery so essential to the work of reducing differences to some acceptable consensus.

The Jacksonian era added to the effectiveness of political parties by introducing the national nominating convention to meet every four years and a system of rewarding the faithful. The former gave the party an opportunity to reorganize and revitalize its spirits. The latter—the spoils system—gave the leadership the power to purchase loyalty and hard work and to punish disloyalty at the same time. Patronage became the circulatory system for the political machine; it supplied both the funds and the workers for the cause at every level. This new politics placed a high premium on the political boss without which the system could not function. The boss needed the national party as much as the national leadership needed him. From the party the boss received money and jobs. In exchange he delivered the votes, but he could continue to do so only if the national leadership met the needs of the people, or at least the promises of the boss. The boss had become the door through which the various interests could bring their needs to the attention of government and the means by which the government could discover those needs.

Into this world the Irish brought their adaptability for politics. Before Jackson's appearance as a presidential candidate, Irish concentrations in New York gave them the power to attract the attention of the city's political leaders. In 1828 they made an important contribution to Jackson's victory, and in the 1830's some Irishmen moved up the political ladder into the state legislature. By the early 1840's the major parties, the Whigs and Democrats, had found the Irish vote too important to ignore.[15] In effect, the Jacksonian era taught the Irish that they could use the basic nature of American democracy to move up from the lower strata of American society. To do this, however, demanded large numbers of voters, concentrated in key states and cities across the country. Until 1835 the Irish functioned in only a few areas, and their numbers did not warrant the influence they were able to exercise upon occasion.

After 1835 a significant change occurred in the movement of the Irish to America. A number of crop failures, coupled with an increasing demand for land that could never be satisfied, caused a number of peasants from the South to sail to America. Unlike their predecessors, these new arrivals brought neither wealth nor education. They remained in the eastern cities. Politicians like Mike Walsh of Tammany Hall realized they possessed one item of value—the right to vote. He brought the newcomers into the Irish ghettos, found them shelter, food, and a place to work at the lowest economic level, that of the ordinary laborer. The numbers increased, and the traffic came more from the South of Ireland than from the North, but the real revolution did not occur until the end of the 1840's. Only then did the Irish in America reach the numbers and cohesiveness of interest so necessary for a group to function successfully in America. An individual could always succeed, but group success demanded both unity of purpose and large numbers.

Meanwhile, Americans learned how to cope with the political innovations of Jackson and his party. At first, the opposition unified around fundamental disagreements with Jackson and his policies, but then it evolved into the Whig party, which employed all of the techniques of the Democrats. By 1840, both fought for control of the electorate with carefully selected candidates, issues, and techniques.

American politics had matured from the relatively primitive narrow battle between groups with little difference of interest, which characterized the early settlement, to the more complex relationships faced by the nation in the 1840's. Numerous groups in widely separated parts of the nation, with differences of opinion on many issues, now struggled for a hearing. All expected the government to respond, and all realized that only through political activity could they expect to be heard. The politician's task was to reconcile these differences and to reduce them to a point where the majority could agree. Into this complex world thousands of Irish men and women rushed in the late 1840's and early 1850's.

CHAPTER 3

The Emergence of Irish-American Nationalism

I *Famine*

L AND and what it produced and not politics formed the heart of Ireland's problems in the early decades of the nineteenth century. Unfortunately, the decisions of English politicians produced O'Connell and his fight to gain the right of Irish Catholics to sit in Parliament. That struggle and O'Connell's later battle to destroy the Act of Union captivated the Irish scene and drove the vital questions of land from the debates of the day. However, neither the Irish nor the English could long ignore the land without inviting disaster. It came in the summer of 1845.

On the eve of the Great Famine the Irish could look back upon a long history with a great degree of pride. The rugged land and damp climate had produced a hearty, witty people who loved life in spite of the long hours of work spent in struggling for mere survival. Fully aware that conditions would not change, they accepted their lot and enjoyed what they had, whenever they could. Their deep respect for Christianity, bordering on blind fanaticism, gave the Irish their only hope—peace and happiness in the next world. Because the Irish believed the word of God and knew the things of this earth had no status in His world, they accepted their fate, did God's will in this world, and waited for their place in the next. With such faith they found joy in adversity.

Leisure moments during good weather were devoted to music and dancing that lasted for hours. The long winter months found small groups, clustered around the fire and the heat, fed by plentiful and cheap stores of peat from the bogs, listening to the stories of the past. With a fresh and full supply of poteen (made at home and, naturally, illegal whiskey) to loosen their tongues, the interest of all would be held by the tales of heroes who had fought and died for Ireland. In this setting they accepted a man for what he was. The stranger received the place before the fire, the seat of honor. They shared what food they had with anyone who came. Hospitality, good manners, and dignity characterized the Irish regardless of their state in life.[1] All considered themselves descendants of kings, and all acted as if they would once more have their rightful place, if only in the next world.

Yet, for all their friendliness and culture, for all their love of music and the traditions of the past, for all their interest in Christianity and the hope for a better life in the next world, the Irish on the eve of the famine had another side. The Penal Codes of the eighteenth century had produced a desperate people. An entire class looked upon the law with such suspicion that they created their own code. Secret societies served as their police, and they punished the sinful landlords and their agents with dreadful savagery. Defiance of the law became a moral necessity, despite the condemnation of church leaders. Coupled to Irish courage, blind daring, love of excitement and conflict of any kind, this disregard for English authority created a nation with a potential for revolution that needed only a spark to drive the masses blindly into the firepower of the British Empire.[2]

Little did anyone realize that empty Irish stomachs would fuel the slaughter. Fortunately for the Irish, the very pressures and virtues that brought them to the point of revolution gave them the strength to survive in the face of the holocaust that was so long in coming and had been too long ignored.

The roots of the Great Famine stretched deep into the Irish land policy of the English government. The British, quite simply and innocently, conceived that policy as a means of preventing pretenders to the throne and enemies of the state from using Ireland as an avenue for attack. The displacing of disloyal Irish lords with loyal Englishmen in the sixteenth century and disloyal Catholics with loyal Protestants in the seventeenth century, effectively destroyed any possibility that Ireland would possess an aristocracy willing to assume a leadership role in her development.

This plantation system produced a new class, the Anglo-Irish Ascendancy, which had its own problems and interests, none of which coincided with Ireland's. The Anglo-Irish lords imitated their more wealthy English counterparts and copied their expensive London living habits. Absenteeism grew as the upper class viewed Ireland only from the point of view of the wealth she could produce to support them in their London townhouses. They gave the management of their estates to overseers and measured an agent's competence by the amount of rents he could extract from the people. England's Irish land policy denied Catholic Ireland the very class that should have provided the leadership necessary to solve her problems, while the Penal Codes effectively limited the development of any middle class that could have filled the void.

The peasant and his land problem wandered across Ireland's stage without direction. The leadership that did emerge in the latter half of the eighteenth century continued to ignore both the people and their problems in favor of the political controversies of Grattan's Parliament and Catholic emancipation. In this situation, the peasant found his own solution to his twin problem of how to pay the rent and feed his family. He raised grain for the former and adopted the potato for the latter, an ideal diet when combined with milk. As long as the potato did not fail and he did not have to use his rent money to feed his family, he could satisfy the landlord's unquenchable thirst for money.

Unfortunately for the Irish peasant, the potato often failed; and he faced the threat of eviction, a virtual sentence of death during a potato failure, as neither he nor his family had any place to go or any means to find work. During those times the peasants solved their problems by forming secret societies that used vicious physical force to prevent eviction. Agrarian warfare followed, and Ireland's misery grew. As long as greedy landlords divided and subdivided holdings in order to squeeze as much as possible from the land, and as long as England denied the peasant any tenure to his holdings or any right to the improvements he made on the land, Ireland would remain literally in or on the verge of war.[3] The potato did little to solve the basic issues.

Two events toward the end of the eighteenth century aggravated these trends. The French Revolution drove the price of grain higher and higher. In response, the Irish put more and more land under grain cultivation. The rents rose, and as long as war continued, the peasant could earn a decent living. With the arrival of peace, however, prices fell and the peasant had to rely more than ever before upon the potato. Gradually his very existence rested upon it.

At the same time, the strange and still unexplained phenomenon of rapid population growth struck the island. Ireland's population statistics are admittedly highly unreliable for the first half of the nineteenth century, but from the available figures most authorities agree that the population increased at the rate of 172 percent between 1789 and 1846—from about three million to over eight million. Some claim the latter figure was closer to nine million on the eve of the famine. Only a small proportion of this increase emigrated to Britain or North America, or anywhere else for that matter, and the vast majority remained to find a way of life in Ireland. No industry, however, existed to absorb them, and there was no middle class to create it even if Ireland had the necessary natural resources. Only the land could absorb the increase, but this accelerated all the evils the Irish land system generated.[4]

Yet as the population jumped from five million in 1800 to six and a half million in 1821 to over eight million in 1841, the peasants still could live. The potato fed them; peat warmed them; the stories, the poteen, and the music kept their spirits alive; and in their minds God in his providence took care of the future. Young people stayed home, and the boys worked in the fields. Girls remained chaste, married at sixteen, and produced offspring every two years with the regularity of a modern family planner. On the eve of the famine, the Irish were undoubtedly happy. In addition to all these joys, O'Connell led his Repeal Association. Its monster meetings fed upon the Irishman's love of excitement, his interest in a fight, his respect for the past, and his undying belief that he would some day possess the dignity bestowed by freedom and nationhood. In spite of its miseries, Irish life in the first years of the 1840's must have been an exciting experience.

The climax came in 1843 in the rapid succession of events that preceded the government's order forbidding the great monster meeting O'Connell organized for Clontarf. The decline, not perceptible at the time, began with O'Connell's capitulation. The Repeal Association slowly waned, and by the spring of 1845 those Irish politicians who now sought a more violent solution to Ireland's problems saw the weaknesses of O'Connell's approach. Then in the summer the crisis of the land, long in coming, suddenly struck with devastating power. Crop failure and famine had appeared before in the 1820's and 1830's, but no one foresaw the events of the late 1840's.

A long siege of rain fell in July, 1845, without any discernible effect on an encouraging potato crop, but in August news that a strange blight had struck the crop in the south of England reached the office of England's Home Secretary.[5] In the next month the same blight destroyed some crops in Ireland, and for the next six weeks conflicting reports concerning the extent of damage arrived in London.

The Conservative party ruled England in the summer of 1845; the Prime Minister Robert Peel reacted with alarm to the reports he received from Ireland. He immediately took certain steps to relieve the rapidly deteriorating situation. In an effort to keep food prices down, and without prior cabinet approval (a sign of how critical the situation appeared to him), Peel ordered the authorities in Ireland to purchase 100,000 pounds of Indian corn. Very early in the crisis he decided not to stop the export of those money crops, the income from which the Irish needed for their rents. This led to a second critical decision, to seek the repeal of the Corn Laws, for only by repealing these laws could Peel import the food necessary to overcome the effect of the famine. Unfortunately for the Irish, England's agrarian interests viewed these laws as their only defense against the slow emergence of the urban industrial society that was gaining control of English life. Peel's decision, in effect, threw the question of the Irish famine into the center of England's hottest political issue. Yet he could not see how he could spend tax money to bring food into Ireland and keep a duty on all food entering the country. His stand split the cabinet, the party, and the country. In effect, these decisions meant that hundreds of thousands of Irish men, women, and children would starve to death, while food was leaving the country and English politicians debated whether they should permit food to enter the country—duty free.

The whole crisis deepened for another reason. The generally accepted philosophy of government at the time—laissez-faire—condemned government interference in economic and social developments. Peel, at least, made an effort to ignore this canon in the winter of 1845–46. His purchase of corn in November and its distribution in February and March, in direct violation of laissez-faire principles, kept the population alive into the spring. But the English nation opposed his policies, which at the same time split his party. He had created a difficult situation at best, and one which led to his downfall on June 25, 1846. The defeat brought the Liberals and Lord John Russell into power, a party and a prime minister with absolute faith in laissez-faire. The policy shift from one of moderate intervention, based upon the magnitude of the crisis, to one of nonintervention, whatever the consequences, came on the eve of another crisis.

The summer of 1846 witnessed the complete collapse of the

potato. The news arrived in England in August. Everyone in power knew the magnitude of the disaster, but Russell refused to modify his opposition to any government assistance. One of the hardest and longest winters in the memory of the people came, food disappeared, and hunger moved across the Irish landscape. The numbers receiving relief jumped from thirty thousand in September to almost a half-million in December. At last Russell could no longer ignore the situation and decided upon a policy of direct relief.

By then, however, the peasants faced an epidemic of fever and numerous other diseases that had spread throughout the land. Left without any other solution, thousands decided to flee. The peasants at long last found the only real solution to their problems. The rush to leave started as early as July and gained momentum as the crisis deepened. Liverpool received hundreds of thousands, and, although the vast majority soon sailed to Canada and America, the city faced the enormous task of caring for them. The continued fumbling by the government and the callous attitude of Russell, his party, and many Englishmen during the winter of 1846–47, intensified the peasant's view of emigration as his only solution.

The peak of the crisis passed in February, 1847, and by the spring and summer of that year some confidence returned when the blight struck less hard. At the same time, the deaths of 1847 and the heavy emigration relieved the pressure on the land. The winter came with much less harsh weather, and when the spring arrived with its new planting season, hopes were higher than they had been for three years. Unfortunately, the blight returned in the summer and fall of 1848 with sufficient fury to smash these hopes. The winter of 1848–49 proved another harsh experience, and not until the summer of 1849 did some relief come.[5] By then, however, the future of Ireland had been charted. Her sons and daughters had discovered the process of scattering en masse to the four corners of the earth.

In the midst of this nightmare, the tone of Ireland's political leaders swung sharply toward radicalism. O'Connell, the Irish moderate member of Parliament, had so dominated the political scene in the first forty years of the century that only his constitutional approach to Ireland's political problems possessed any force in the period between the attempted revolution in 1803 until the denial by the authorities of a permit for the Clontarf meeting in 1843. This and O'Connell's refusal to lead any violent response to it strengthened the growth of the Young Irelanders. This new movement used the weekly newspaper, the *Nation*, as a vehicle for expressing more radical demands and solutions to Ireland's problems. They demanded action.

O'Connell still dominated the Irish scene at the start of the famine, but the magnitude of the disaster and his own inability to convince Parliament to act caused the now seventy-year-old man to find some solace in a trip to Rome. He died in May, 1847, in Genoa, never reaching the city in which he expected to regain his health and strength.

His death, the circumstances surrounding it, the immensity of the famine, and the insensitivity of the British government combined to end any hope for the future that may have existed in Ireland. The constitutional approach as a solution to Ireland's problems died with O'Connell and control of Irish politics shifted into the hands of the *Nation*'s proprietors and the party of young men they supported. Secretly and carefully they laid plans to employ physical force to drive the hated British from Ireland's suffering shores. However, the spy system, controlled from Dublin Castle, the seat of British government in Ireland, and fed by English gold, discovered the plot and landed the planners in prison before the outbreak occurred. Only William Smith O'Brien at the head of a small half-starved band of followers mounted an armed attack upon a force of police, but his folly ended in his capture. Ireland simply was not ready for revolution in 1848.[7] The famine had destroyed her will to resist, and the people would not follow a totally hopeless cause. The movement died quickly. In the late summer and fall of 1848, the blight returned, and the peasants continued their prayers, not for food or freedom, but for salvation. Only death remained certain.

By 1851 the results of the famine were showing clearly. First, the upward spiral of population was reversed. In the six years from 1845 to 1851, two million people had either perished or fled the island. Never again would Ireland regain the old rate of population growth. Second, the famine dealt a paralyzing blow to Ireland's agricultural system in which most tenants worked small holdings and thus hastened the construction of a system based upon larger units. The marginal existence of the prefamine years continued, but these larger units meant that never again would so many persons suffer such deprivations. Eventually, this change in the size of holdings also had a profound effect upon the political life of England, for although the famine literally exhausted the people and few cared about political agitation for thirty years, after its occurrence, the peasants occupied a much stronger position than before the events of the late 1840's. Finally, the famine forced the acceptance of the only solution to the size of Ireland's population—emigration—especially to America. From 1845 to 1900 four million Irishmen sailed across the Atlantic to build an Irish enclave within America which eventually surpassed in numbers and in power the nation left behind.[8]

The Young Ireland movement also had its effects. The rashness of its attempt at revolution in the face of hopeless odds killed extremist political activity in Ireland for some time. What leadership Ireland possessed for the next decade concentrated upon parliamentary changes, while the Young Irelanders, forced to leave Ireland and dispersed to the four corners of the world, slowly made their way to America. By the middle of the 1850's Ireland's future had sailed across the Atlantic. The famine sent the masses to America. The Young Ireland party and its abortive revolution provided their leaders.[9]

II Irish America

The "famine Irish" arrived in America in possession of few things of any value, but with an intense love and an equally intense hate. The Irish came in a state of shock. They had not wanted to leave Ireland. They did so only to flee death. The basic human desire to live drove them from their beloved hills and valleys, from the poteen, the music, and the storytelling. When they got to America, their yearning for the past naturally led them to settle in Irish ghettos. In the crowded streets of America's great cities they could recall together their beloved land and its rich heritage. Afraid of the wide open spaces of America's farm belt, they found conditions in the ghettos of America's great cities more conducive to their needs. There they created a romantic picture of the Emerald Isle that soon possessed no resemblance to the land they had left.

The peasant's hatred of England equaled his love of Ireland; America intensified both. The bitter experience of the famine, the passage across the Atlantic, the loneliness of the New World, and the utterly bewildering experience of the city beyond the safety of their ghetto shattered the immigrant's confidence. Because he laid all of his troubles at the feet of England, the constant awareness of these experiences fueled an insatiable thirst for vengeance. Someday he would collect his just debts; but, meanwhile, he would stand ready at a moment's notice to move against those that had created his misery.[10]

When the famine Irish arrived in America, they found a large number of friendly faces. Some had been born in Ireland; others were descendants of Irish-born parents. Although the relatively small number of prefamine Catholic immigrants had limited their ability to influence the nation's life as a group, many individuals had risen above the general population, and a few families played prominent roles. Those who possessed wealth, education, or both, quickly improved their position in America's political, social, and economic life. One found these Irishmen in literature, both as writers and dealers in books, in journalism, in the legal and teaching professions, and in medicine. At the same time, the Irish had clearly emerged as a potent political force at the local level, especially in certain large eastern cities. The campaign battles of New York during the 1830's clearly foreshadowed the future role of the Irish in that state.[11] Yet the coming of the famine Irish changed the whole character of the Irish in America. In turn, many Americans reacted by exhibiting little friendly interest in the newcomers.

In the years immediately preceding the Great Famine, which coincided with the Jacksonian era, Americans focused their inherent reforming instincts upon such issues as strengthening democracy, creating a public school system to educate the children of the common man toward good citizenship, abolishing slavery, and restructuring America's prisons. A few went as far as constructing, in their worlds, the perfect community. These efforts generated considerable discussion of the basic nature of America and caused some to reflect upon the Irish migration. Slowly the old nativist tendencies of the Federalist period reemerged as many Americans believed that an overabundance of foreigners and Catholics would destroy the basic fabric of the nation. Antiforeign and anti-Catholic mobs attacked convents and Catholic schools. Riots occurred in Philadelphia and New York during the 1840's; in both instances, the Irish participated and upheld the side of their religion. The great flow of famine Irish in the late 1840's only intensified this nativist animosity. The new immigrants encountered much bigotry and hatred.[12] Unfortunately for later Irish-Negro relations, some leaders of the movement to grant freedom to the black man soon stood in the forefront of the battle to deny those same rights to Irish Catholics.

In the decade of the 1850's the Irish continued to arrive in large numbers, year after year. Both lower- and upper-class Americans came more and more to fear the effect of such a large influx upon American political institutions. Consequently, their prejudice and bigotry increased. This unfavorable reception, coupled with the immigrants' basic loneliness and yearning for Ireland, only intensified their search for safety in numbers. Irish enclaves in Boston, New York, and Philadelphia continued to grow. These sharply defined geographic ghettos soon assumed the characteristics of all slums—filth, disease, crime, and a population addicted to liquor. The local political "boss" marshaled these Irish forces, and the popular belief that they voted as a bloc for whomever the "boss" favored convinced many Americans by the mid-1850's that the Irish threatened democracy, the free enterprise system, and the nation itself. In his own little world, confronted by hostility in every direction, the ex-peasant developed a sense of inferiority, a sensitiveness to criticism, and a yearning for respectability.

Yet he soon discovered in America he did not have to be poor; he did not have to be shunted away from the mainstream of society. In America, the land of opportunity, he could achieve respectability; but it took time. The realization that he could not improve his lot immediately forced him to rationalize his failure. His hatred of England gave him the answer. His ancestry handicapped him. America would accept him, as she had accepted the prefamine Irish, if only the ex-peasant could convince the average American that English policies had made him poor, dirty, crime-infested, and liquor-prone—that the Anglo-Irish Ascendancy, those English-Protestant transplants who had ruled Ireland for two hundred years, and the obnoxious land system had cause the plight of the Irish in America. The peasant could prove this, if only Ireland could gain her freedom.

Paradoxically, the immigrant's desire to earn the privilege of being called an American produced his peculiar brand of Irish-American nationalism. Events and experiences in Ireland provided the masses, the leaders, the loves and hates for this new nationalism. American experiences supplied the cause for its existence. The immigrant became a marginal man, neither Irish nor American, "whose principal literature was hostile to England, whose heroes and martyrs were either political prisoners or executed felons, and whose every aspiration and hope was at variance with the established order of things in the land which they had left."[13]

The ex-peasant in America had no real desire to return to Ireland, and few did. No hope awaited him there. If he were to find a new life, it could only be in the New World; but that embroiled him in direct involvement in the Anglo-Irish struggle. By the end of the 1850's the Irish in America began to stir. The remnants of the Young Ireland movement had spent the decade creating plans to forge the Irish in America into a powerful force which they could use in the centuries-old Anglo-Irish struggle. At first they founded newspapers to reach the masses, organized lecture tours, held picnics and parades, and started to use the power of the vote to embarrass the British government whenever possible.

In this work the Young Irelanders had some precedents. In the early 1840's Irish-Americans participated in movements to support O'Connell's struggle to gain Ireland's right to her own Parliament, and in 1846, they developed plans to intervene in the Oregon dispute with England. Two years later Irish Republican clubs appeared in New York City in support of the Young Ireland movement.

Soon English statesmen became concerned about the effect of returning veterans from the Mexican War upon Irish-American plans to invade Canada. The Irish Revolution of 1848 forced the United States to become officially involved when the British arrested a number of American citizens in Ireland. What would become a most familiar story as the century unfolded caused the American Secretary of State James Buchanan and his minister in London, George Bancroft, a great deal of difficulty as Irish rebels with American citizenship found themselves in jail without the right of trial by jury. They demanded that America intervene and assure their freedom, and after a considerable exchange the British finally agreed to release them if they left Ireland. A few years later the Irish in America showed their persistence when the British became involved in the Crimean conflict with Russia. Some Irishmen offered to send arms and volunteers to Russia, while one group in Boston planned to send a force directly to Ireland.[14]

All of these efforts failed, however, and for many reasons. First of all, the newly arrived immigrants were concerned about their own problems and could devote little time or effort to any serious effort to help Ireland. Second, the million that arrived in the period from 1845 to 1855 disrupted many of the old patterns and neighborhoods and created immense problems of organization and assimilation. In addition, Ireland itself was relatively quiet during the 1850's, and the radical solution to her problems gained few adherents during the decade. Finally, too many voices spoke to the Irish masses in America and often caused confusion. Not until these things changed could the Irish consolidate their power and bring it to bear upon England's relations with Ireland and America's relations with England.

Meanwhile, the exiled Young Irelanders prepared for the future. In 1857 John O'Mahoney formed the Fenian movement in America and then tied this body to the Irish Revolutionary Brotherhood in Ireland under the leadership of James Stephens. Starting slowly, this new organization pointed toward the future when the Irish would possess the power and freedom to act. Its leaders had to wait until the close of America's Civil War.[15]

CHAPTER 4

Irish Soldiers

I   Civil War

IN the 1850's Americans gradually drifted toward war as events and tragically inadequate leadership permitted the emergence of two separate and distinct mentalities. The issues that divided the nation had burned for years, but until 1852 a series of events had masked them. In that year the false sense of unity that had followed the Compromise of 1850 began to evaporate with the election of Franklin Pierce, the rise of nativism and the Know-Nothing party, the reaction to the Fugitive Slave Law, and the publication of *Uncle Tom's Cabin*. In the years that followed, the breakdown of unity continued, aided by the growing power of the radical Abolitionists, expansionist feelings in the South, and the passage of the Kansas-Nebraska Act, which led to the demise of the Whigs and to virtual civil war in Kansas. The appearance of the Republicans and their relative success in the campaign of 1856 was followed by the ill-managed presidency of James Buchanan. The Dred Scott decision, with its declaration of the unconstitutionality of the Missouri Compromise, and the Lincoln-Douglas debates, split the nation further. Bitter memories of such events as Brooks's attack on Sumner and John Brown's raid on Harpers Ferry kept the split from healing. By 1860 the nation stood on the edge of catastrophe.[1]

The Irish carefully watched this mounting fury because the issue at the center of the storm, the status of the Negroes, meant much to them. They had no love for the Negro, nor did America's blacks have any love for them. Many Americans considered Negroes of more value than "paddies," and the immigrants discovered this as soon as they landed, often from the attitude of the Negroes themselves. Much of this antagonism existed because the Irish could find work only at the lowest economic level and often had to do what was considered too dangerous for the more valuable Negro. Any movement to free large numbers of slaves, therefore, earned their bitter opposition, since it would only increase competition for jobs at that level and complicate the already difficult task of earning a living.

During the 1850's this situation led to a number of battles between Irish and Negro laborers in cities from New York to Milwaukee. At the same time, Irish leaders, including members of the Roman Catholic hierarchy, condemned Abolitionists; only a rare Irish editor or lecturer openly condemned slavery. The ex-peasant particularly disliked those who fought with great moral indignation for the rights of Negroes but denied these same rights to immigrants.[2]

In that atmosphere the Irish naturally gravitated toward the southern view on the slave issue, while ignoring any political party that smacked of abolitionism and bitterly condemned "Black Republicans" for assuming the mantle of Know-Nothingism. As the Civil War approached, the Irish in effect supported the Democratic party, which would soon disintegrate, and that side of an issue which would soon become untenable. Yet by 1860, the Irish had gained considerable status above the position they had occupied ten years before.

In that critical election year almost 2 million Irishmen lived in the United States in a total population of 31.5 million, roughly 7 percent of the white population. As there were more males than females among the Irish than among the general population, these numbers had even greater political significance; and although they were scattered in every state (827 in Florida to 498,072 in New York; .009 percent of the population in North Carolina to 15.7 percent in Massachusetts), the Irish remained concentrated in politically important cities, both large and small.[3] Peculiar local circumstances gave them significant political power in many cities; but their large numbers, coupled with the growing second generation, meant that the Irish in America already potentially represented one of the country's largest pressure groups.

Party men showed an interest in the Irish for a second reason. The trip across the Atlantic, still vivid in their minds, the loneliness of their arrival, and the bitter Know-Nothing attacks of the mid-1850's made this particular ethnic group fully conscious of their Irishism. Constant harangues of politicians urging the Irish to think, act, and vote as Irishmen and the arguments of the Young Ireland political refugees that the ex-peasant should neither ignore the old country nor forget his hatred of England combined to create strong feelings of cohesiveness. The parish priest's insistence that they maintain their Catholicism in spite of an alien world and the Irish press that served as the vehicle for communication kept that element of mutual interest alive. Combined with their numbers, this cohesiveness of sentiment and purpose created an enormous political potential.

As an awareness of Irish power grew toward the end of the 1850's, American politicians played a curious game in the face of serious divisions. Stephen A. Douglas, a contender for the Democratic presidential nomination, traveled through the North seeking to mend his political fences, while the Republicans like William Seward and Abraham Lincoln worked to deflate stories that their party possessed no sense of moderation, nor any willingness to make concessions to southern sympathies.

These attempts to mold the Democrats and Republicans into parties that could bridge the widening gaps in American life evaporated at their respective party conventions. The Democrats first met in Charleston, South Carolina, but soon hopelessly ended in a deadlock. Two weeks later the remnants of the Whigs and Know-Nothings formed the Constitution Union party and nominated John Bell of Tennessee and Edward Everett of Massachusetts for president and vice-president, respectively. The Republicans met in Chicago, passed a conservative and moderate platform, and nominated "Honest Abe." Yet it was obvious to all that Lincoln led a northern party. By June the Democrats reassembled, this time in Baltimore, but once again split into two factions. The regulars nominated Stephen A. Douglas, while the bolters nominated John C. Breckinridge of Kentucky. No real consensus existed on the national scene. The inevitable had resulted. If, as some have said, the major parties of the 1850's reflected at best a loose merging of state and local interests, it was clear by September, 1860, that neither leadership nor a specific program had emerged to unite these various interests on the national level.[4] Faction politics had returned to Washington, as a rudderless nation simply drifted into the inevitable clash.

The election campaign did nothing to stop this drift. Democrats accused the Republicans of a sinister plan to destroy slavery, while Republicans argued that they favored a moderate position. The campaign only reflected the division in the nation. Lincoln and

Douglas ran in the North, Bell and Breckinridge in the South. The results gave Lincoln the electoral vote but only 39.9 percent of the popular vote. The split of the Democrats into northern and southern parties over the issue of slavery gave the Republicans and the North control of the White House and the nation.

The Irish played an important, but losing, role in this battle. Although Republicans made some attempts to organize the Irish, few voted for Lincoln, while in the North the vast majority of the Irish vote went to Douglas and the Democrats. Those in the South for the most part went to Breckinridge in spite of a large and strong following for Douglas. In both sections, the concept of the Union remained strong, and during the period between the election and the inaugural, as the nation rapidly drifted toward war, the Irish urged all to work for peace.[5] Yet, when the war finally came, they supported their cause, the Union or the Confederacy, depending upon where they lived.

The Civil War disrupted much of American life, but it also produced some positive results, especially for the Irish. Prior to the famine, the reputation of the Irish in most parts of the country had rested on the activity of individuals. Not until the 1850's did Americans on the whole come to know the Irish as a group, only to attribute certain unfavorable characteristics to them. On the eve of the war the Irish knew that they still did not belong. The war gave them the opportunity to earn a new reputation and to take another step toward becoming Americans.

The war inspired large numbers of Irishmen to enlist in local militia units, while others followed the appeals of popular Irish heroes and joined Irish units. Soon Irish regiments from various states appeared in the Union army. The Irish Ninth and the Twenty-eighth, both from Massachusetts, carried green flags into battle. Colonel John McCuskey recruited Irish for the Fifteenth Maine, while other "paddies" filled the ranks of the Ninth Connecticut, the Tenth New Hampshire, and New York's "Fighting Sixty-ninth." Together with the Sixty-third and Eighty-third, the Sixty-ninth formed the famous Irish Brigade. Pennsylvania also had an Irish Sixty-ninth which fought at Gettysburg while another Irish unit, the One-hundred and Sixteenth, fought in numerous battles. Other regiments came from Indiana, Missouri, Ohio, Wisconsin, and Illinois.

Irish-Americans produced officers as well as men. Michael

Corcoran, James Shields, Thomas Meagher (the Young Irelander of the 1848 rebellion), and second-generation Philip H. Sheridan all rose to high rank. Hundreds of captains, majors, and colonels filled various positions in the Union army, and many earned respectable positions after the war on the strength of their army careers. St. Clair A. Mulholland, for instance, left the service as a major general of volunteers to become Philadelphia's police chief. In all, over 144,000 native-born Irish served in the Union forces.

At the start of the war only eighty-five thousand Irish-Americans lived in the South, and almost without exception they supported the Confederacy. Off they marched to war to fight the Yankees in units from Louisiana, Virginia, Alabama, Tennessee, North Carolina, and South Carolina. As in the North, many Irishmen rose to a high rank in the Confederate army. General Patrick Cleburne commanded the Fifth Confederate Regiment, composed mostly of immigrants who had settled in Alabama, while Patrick Moore led the First Regiment Infantry, Virginia Volunteers and left the service as a brigadier general.[6]

In both the North and the South the Irish earned a reputation for gallantry as they fought on the eastern and western fronts and in battles from Bull Run to Missionary Ridge. At times, Irish units fought each other for control of key terrain, and in the lulls between conflict each could hear the sound of Irish songs from the opposing lines.

The Irish, like other members of the Union army, also received a share of some bad publicity. Hardly well disciplined, Union troops were known for their constant brawling, drinking, and running from battle, and the Irish were no exceptions. Yet the biggest negative mark on their record during the war occurred hundreds of miles from the front lines.

By the spring of 1863 Congress realized that Lincoln could fill the ranks of the Union army only with conscription and on March 3 passed America's first draft law. The power created by this unfortunate piece of legislation soon fell into the hands of politicians, who used it for their own purposes. Soon their actions aroused great animosity. The act also permitted a draftee to escape his obligation by a payment of $300 in cash or by furnishing a substitute, which meant the burden obviously fell upon the poor. This infuriated the Irish, especially because the Emancipation Proclamation had converted the war into a fight to free the slaves.

The draft and the proclamation forced the Irish to fight for something that would greatly increase the competition for the work they performed. Riots soon broke out in various cities, but the worst occurred in New York.

The first drawing in New York took place in July, 1863, and produced a draft list containing a large number of Irish names. This caused the ex-peasants to explode, especially because their dislike of Negroes had been sorely tested when Negroes helped to break a strike by Irish longshoremen and stevedores. In a town in which the highest authorities had exhibited numerous southern sympathies, the Irish rioted for four days, burning the draft office, attacking police, destroying a Negro orphan asylum, and killing Negroes and Chinese. Anywhere from eighteen to seventy-four persons died. Only the urgings of the clergy and the arrival of troops ended the disorders. In a unanimous voice the nation condemned the disorders, and many felt that the Irish as a group had suffered a severe blow. Other voices soon explained that the police, mostly Irish, fought the disorders and that Irish priests, including the archbishop of New York, helped to limit the damage.[7] Hence the draft riots did not destroy the impact of the behavior of the Irish in uniform, which had contributed greatly toward their acceptance as a group, and the image of the Irishman, who was also a good American, continued to spread.

II *Changing Forces*

While the Irish spilled their blood to insure acceptance, America's relations with England deteriorated. On the eve of the war, America experienced the best relations she had had with the Mother Country in many years. Not since the Franco-American naval disputes of 1799 had the British been so friendly, and when the war started that relationship remained unchanged as most Englishmen, both official and unofficial, saw the war as an effort to end slavery.[8] The English soon shifted their opinions, however, and gradually viewed the conflict in terms of self-determination. In that context they quickly looked upon the South with greater favor. In many ways this was only a natural outgrowth of other influences. The upper classes of England had much in common with the planter aristocracy of the Confederacy, for instance, and as a group they detested the vulgar democracy of the North. In addition, England had some very obvious economic and strategic reasons for hoping the rebels would gain their independence, but none of these was strong enough to cause Britain to abandon an official policy of neutrality.

In spite of her official stand, a number of specific incidents arose to sour England's relations with the Union. Americans, for instance, bitterly resented England's proclamation of neutrality which in effect recognized a state of war between the Union and the Confederacy. Shortly afterward, an American man-of-war stopped a British mail steamer, the *Trent*, on the high seas and removed two Confederate agents from her decks. The Union reacted with hysterical joy, while England exploded. This case unfortunately lingered until December, 1861, when Lincoln's cabinet agreed that the Confederate agents had to be released to British jurisdiction. Within six months of that decision arose the question of a Confederate navy being built in English shipyards. In July, 1862, the *Alabama* slipped out of England and along with other commercial raiders eventually destroyed 250 Union ships. In 1863 news arrived that English yards were building powerful ironclad steam vessels, armed with wrought-iron rams and 9-inch rifled guns. Though in this case the British government acted to prevent these vessels from falling into Confederate hands, this action did not halt the American people's rising Anglophobia, which by the summer of 1863 clearly threatened to erupt into war.[9]

During these same years conditions in Ireland moved in a direction that would greatly influence both the Irish in America and Anglo-American relations. Because the Great Famine and the failures of the Young Ireland movement had exhausted the revolutionary element in Irish national life, the 1850's witnessed the return to milder methods of agitation. In 1850 Charles Gavan Duffy founded the Tenant Right League which demanded fair rents, fixity of tenure, and freedom for the tenant to sell his interest (improvements) in his holding. Duffy believed the Irish could gain these if they developed an independent party in Parliament. Such a party almost emerged in the general elections of 1852, when roughly forty Irish members declared in favor of such rights; but this unity soon evaporated as some members acted more in the interest of their own careers than in the interest of the peasants. As the decade of the 1850's ended, the failure of the constitutional approach to Ireland's grievances caused a gradual shift of interest to the more radical and violent elements in Irish political life.[10] James

Stephens and his newly founded Irish Revolutionary Brotherhood stood ready to take advantage of the change in opinion. Slowly and methodically the brotherhood organized the small farmers and laborers, the clerks and shop assistants. In the midst of America's Civil War, Stephens decided the time for a visit to America had arrived.

In the summer of 1863 the rising power of the Irish in America converged with the deterioration of Anglo-American relations and with the return in Ireland of the radicals to Irish politics. The Irish at home and in America, cheered by the growing animosity between London and Washington, viewed war between the two nations as the guarantee to the success of an Irish drive for independence. News from Ireland of a growing feeling in favor of a violent attempt at independence further aroused their hopes. Both developments came just as the Irish-Americans realized their power. Thousands of Irish-born Americans now had military training and experience. A large body of capable officers stood ready to use their hard-earned knowledge for the good of the Emerald Isle. In addition, both officers and men believed a successful independence movement in Ireland would greatly add to their rising pride in themselves and their growing respectability in America.

III   *War Against England*

The link-up of these developments rapidly formed in 1863. From the start of the Fenian movement in America, John O'Mahoney, who emigrated from Ireland in the 1850's, ran the organization with arbitrary and dictatorial powers. This worked well enough as long as the movement remained, relatively speaking, small in numbers and underfinanced. From the start, the IRB leadership—both in Ireland and America—entertained the hope that in addition to contributions of both money and moral support, the Irish in America would provide a military organization which would stand forever ready to take advantage of England's difficulties with other nations and, thus, help to gain Ireland her well-deserved freedom. The Civil War rapidly increased the possibility of producing the kind of military machine Stephens and O'Mahoney wanted; furthermore, federal officials had deliberately played upon these dreams when they had recruited Irishmen both in America and in Ireland for the Union regiments.

Such encouragement spread these hopes throughout the Irish

ranks of the Union army during 1861 and 1862 and created a situation which demanded the reorganization of the Fenian movement. Stephens' visit to the United States further increased this possibility, and O'Mahoney agreed to hold a convention in Chicago on November 3, 1863. The eighty-two delegates from twelve states, the District of Columbia and the armies of the Cumberland, the Potomac, and the Tennessee established a procedure for electing the head centre (president), a central treasurer, and an advisory cabinet of five men. The new organization rapidly increased the size of the brotherhood, and when they gathered for their second convention in Cincinnati in January, 1865, the number of delegates had climbed to 348 and the Circles (local branches) to 273. The convention reelected O'Mahoney to the top post of head centre, but increased the number of his cabinet to ten and elected men of action to these seats. Within months the new cabinet, contrary to O'Mahoney's advice, voted to increase the number of paid organizers.[11] By the spring of 1865 Irishmen in many parts of America stood ready to move against England.

Two events occurred in April, 1865, that increased the hopes of those who wanted immediate action. On the second day of the month, Gen. Robert E. Lee evacuated Richmond. A week later he surrendered to Gen. Ulysses S. Grant. The war was over after four long and bitter years. President Lincoln announced his policy of leniency toward the defeated states and toured the ex-capital of Richmond, but he returned to Washington only to receive an assassin's bullet.

The end of the war suddenly freed thousands of Irish troops for service in Ireland, and IRB organizers accelerated their recruiting efforts, for they now could work among ex-Confederate troops as well as among ex-Unionists. The number of Circles rapidly increased in the late spring and summer of 1865, and demands for action grew louder and louder. The cabinet, using this clamor as a pretext, finally authorized, over O'Mahoney's objections, the calling of a new convention to meet in Philadelphia to perfect plans for the end of British rule in Ireland. Over six hundred delegates arrived for the opening session, but like so many Irish political movements the convention ended in division. The delegates eventually rewrote the IRB's constitution, but that struggle split the brotherhood into two factions. O'Mahoney led one, while William Roberts led what became known as the Senate faction. Each completed plans for separate invasions of Canada.[12]

The second event, the assassination of Lincoln, had no immediate effect upon the Fenians. However, when it quickly became evident in the summer and fall of 1865 that a battle would form over Reconstruction, the whole picture of the possible Irish role in postwar America changed. President Andrew Johnson wanted to implement Lincoln's mild policies, but the Republican-controlled Congress proposed a policy of harsh repression. The division became clear in December, 1865, when Congress reconvened and refused to accept senators and representatives elected according to Johnson's plan. Congress then studied the problem and in early 1866 passed a series of bills designed to guarantee the Negro the right to vote, a guarantee which would insure a base for the Republican party in the south. Johnson fought this approach and by the summer of 1866 had decided to form the National Union party to rally support for his program in the 1866 congressional elections. That decision meant that Johnson would have to make deliberate appeals to specific interests groups to insure victory for those candidates who supported his policies. In short, the political campaign of 1866 for control of Congress (Democrats, Republicans, and National Unionists) played into the hands of the Fenians. It gave them the opportunity to use the power of the Irish vote to force political concessions from the Johnson administration.

At this critical point the Irish were aided by the extreme bitterness that characterized the complex world of Anglo-American relations. In the course of the Civil War, some Confederate forces had used the Canadian border as a sanctuary from which to launch attacks upon the Union. Consequently, at the close of the war some Americans demanded the forceful annexation of Canada. Coupled with the feeling against England, which the *Alabama* claims had crystallized, this animosity against Canada tended to increase Fenian hopes for their own success against Canada, which Seward and the administration in general actively encouraged. The secretary of state and his diplomatic assistants used Fenian activities as a lever to force English acceptance of American claims against her.[13] Thus, the needs of America's politicians as well as her diplomats gave the Irish in America the leverage to plan freely and openly for the invasion of Ireland and Canada. The situation quickly led to problems that involved the English, the Americans, and the Irish.

In 1865 Irish veterans of America's Civil War arrived in Ireland to participate in the planned revolution, while their colleagues in the IRB remained in America to collect the funds for the necessary arms. The British had suspected for some time that the Fenians would attempt to arouse the peasants at the close of America's Civil War. Reports from British diplomats in America to that effect led the government to pass a coercion law that permitted Irish authorities to make arrests on mere suspicion and without the right of trial by jury. As a result, a number of Americans found themselves in English jails. Their fellow revolutionaries in America immediately demanded American diplomatic intervention on behalf of these citizens, arguing that only their immediate release would remove this British insult to the flag. Upon making inquiries, the American minister in London soon became involved in a full discussion of England's ancient law, "Once an Englishman, always an Englishman."[14] In the end, these arrests and the resulting negotiations only intensified Anglo-American difficulties.

Meanwhile, a more alarming situation from the British viewpoint occurred in America where the Fenians publicly plotted for the overthrow of English rule. Bonds were sold, picnics held, and lectures given as the movement touched every Irish community in America. Official and unofficial diplomatic efforts were made to have the American government stop such displays, but neither Secretary of State William Seward nor President Johnson would intervene.

Anglo-American relations went from bad to worse in 1866, after the two Fenian factions completed their plans for the conquest of Canada. The split in October, 1865, had delayed the shipment of the arms necessary for the Civil War veterans in Ireland to overthrow English rule, and the Irish leaders in Dublin had to postpone the planned revolution. Meanwhile, those Fenians loyal to the leadership of William Roberts decided to attack Canada without coordinating their plans with either the O'Mahoney wing or the Stephens leadership in Ireland. Roberts, who later served in the United States Congress, had by this time formed an elaborate Irish republic in the heart of New York City with all of the trimmings of a recognized government, including a war department and "armies in the field." After much public fanfare, that republic mobilized these "armies" in the spring of 1866 for the long awaited attack on Canada. O'Mahoney, meanwhile, with much less public display, had decided to mount his effort against Canada and actually did so before Roberts could complete his plans. In April, 1866, his wing attempted to capture Campo Bello Island. Seward intervened, however, and the invasion collapsed. Six weeks later, Roberts' faction marched into Canada across the Niagara frontier in a coordinated, many-pronged attack. This time Seward and Johnson refused to intervene and waited four days to issue a neutrality proclamation.

In early June the administration viewed Roberts' invasion of Canada from a difficult position. Seward wanted to use the Fenian activity in his negotiations with the British on the *Alabama* claims, while Johnson wanted Irish voters to support his National Union party which would then run candidates in the November elections for Congress. For these reasons he and his cabinet refused to issue a neutrality proclamation until the so-called invading army had returned to American soil after their defeat by the Canadians. The proclamation forced American authorities to arrest them and confiscate their arms. This action in turn generated bitter Irish complaints about the American government. Some accused the administration of encouraging the Irish to purchase arms and then betraying the movement at the last moment. Numerous Irish journals denounced Johnson as a tool of the British government, hardly a proper title for one who needed Irish votes. The attorney-general quickly ordered all cases against Fenians dropped and all confiscated arms returned to their owners. He also provided, at government expense, transportation for all Fenians who wanted to go home. In addition, the president appealed to Canada on behalf of Fenians captured during the invasion. An American consul actually hired lawyers to defend these prisoners. These attempts to cater to the Irish vote, however, did not solve President Johnson's problems. The Radical Republicans gained control of Congress in November, and the precarious political balance that had encouraged Irish hopes evaporated somewhat.[15]

The revolt in Ireland finally came in the following year, but more than adequately prepared British authorities quickly suppressed the effort. As in 1848, no mass support developed. Once again radicalism temporarily disappeared as the dominant political force in the country. At the same time, the political situation in America rapidly changed. The Radical Republicans passed the famous Reconstruction Acts in March, 1867, and eventually instituted impeachment proceedings against President Johnson. The political balance now leaned heavily in their favor. Meanwhile, Seward made some progress on the Alabama claims; and although Anglophobia did not disappear, the strength of the bitterness of the previous two years lessened.

In 1868 the Republicans nominated Grant for the presidency. He won easily, and his victory marked the end of any significant political leverage for the Irish. Although Grant made a somewhat serious effort to attract Irish voters and gained some of them, his election rested essentially upon a broad alliance of interest groups which did not include the Irish. They could, therefore, expect few concessions. In addition, the diplomatic situation changed dramatically on January 14, 1869, when the United States and England signed the Johnson-Clarendon Convention which settled the Alabama claims. Unfortunately for America, the Senate rejected this convention one month after Grant entered office, but Hamilton Fish, the new secretary of state, entered upon his duties determined to settle all complaints with England. His patient work eventually led to the Treaty of Washington in 1871. As a result, Anglo-American animosities decreased, and America's diplomats no longer needed the Fenian threat to force concessions from England.[16]

While these events occurred in America, the Liberal party won England's general elections in the summer of 1868. On the eve of the new Parliament, William Gladstone became prime minister for the first time and united the Liberals on the question of the disestablishment of the Church of Ireland. When Parliament passed this act in 1869, Gladstone had removed one of Catholic Ireland's more serious grievances. In the following year Parliament passed the Irish Land Act, which applied the chief provisions of the Ulster tenant rights to the whole of Ireland. Charles Gavan Duffy's dream had come true. It was not perfect, of course, as it did not confer security of tenure nor end competitive rents; but at least it showed that parliamentary action could gain some protection against arbitrary eviction and compensation for improvements paid for by the tenants. The failure of the radicals and Gladstone's endorsement of Irish complaints gave Irish political leadership in the 1870's to those who saw the parliamentary method as the solution to Ireland's problems.

By 1870 the conditions that had produced the Fenian movement in America no longer existed, and the movement itself slowly faded away. One last effort, however, was made in May, 1870, when Gen.

John O'Neill attempted to invade Canada from New Hampshire. A United States marshal arrested O'Neill, and his army evaporated. The movement which began with such high hopes ended as a tragicomedy which in no way adequately reflected its accomplishments.

Prior to 1858 the Irish influenced America only at the local level, and seldom, if at all, did they speak with one voice on specific issues and policies. The Fenians proved that the Irish in America could be organized and that they could use their power at the ballot boxes to force Washington to listen and respond to their demands. Not all Irish-Americans agreed with the Fenian definition of how Washington could meet those needs, especially in their fight against England; but all recognized what the Fenians had accomplished. By intensifying the Irish-American's awareness of himself and by focusing that awareness upon the attainment of Ireland's freedom, this nationalist movement created a new and effective pressure group at the national level. No longer would native Americans see the Irish chiefly as crime-infested, disease-ridden, whiskey-drinking inhabitants of slums. Unwittingly, the ex-peasant had discovered that the secret to success for any group in pluralistic America lay in cohesiveness and numbers.

CHAPTER 5

Quiet Years of Assimilation

I   *Increasing Economic Power*

THE failure of the Fenians and the reduction of Ireland's grievances which followed Gladstone's appointment as prime minister marked a temporary end to radical domination of Irish-American nationalists and thus permitted the Irish of the 1870's to devote their energies to the more immediate task of finding their place in their new world. In this regard, they had certain advantages over their predecessors.

In the first place, their experiences during the Civil War changed the nature of their organizations. From the beginning, the Irish, like other immigrants, established formal associations through which they hoped to help each other as well as themselves. As early as 1771 they formed the Society of the Friendly Sons of Saint Patrick for the Relief of Emigrants from Ireland to Philadelphia; the society was formally incorporated in 1792. A similar society appeared in Charleston, South Carolina, in 1791, and numerous others followed in New York, Brooklyn, Rochester, Toledo, Chicago, and Saint Louis. By the 1850's the Irish supported various beneficial, literary, and social organizations in towns across the country.

In these the lost and bewildered immigrant found companionship and that essential sense of belonging that he had left behind. These organizations also served as a convenient tool to gather the faithful together for what became their major holiday, March 17, and for what became the traditional means of celebrating it, the parade in honor of Saint Patrick. Wherever one found Irishmen one encountered their organizations and a celebration on March 17. Even in Petersburg, Virginia, a sleepy southern town of fifteen thousand in the 1850's, a Hibernian Society existed and celebrated that day with an appropriate dinner and appropriate toasts.[1]

Prior to the Civil War, such societies remained fundamentally local in nature and appeal. The first real attempt to create a national social organization came in 1856 with the Irish Emigrant Aid Convention in Buffalo, New York. Called to organize the Irish on the national level for the purpose of moving the ex-peasants away from the evils of city life and into the healthy world of the farm, the convention, supported by many Catholic clergymen, attracted about eighty delegates. Although they adopted a fairly elaborate plan to fulfill their dreams, the group never met again.[2] In the mid-1850's no real body of public sentiment existed among the Irish for either such a plan or such a national organization.

The Civil War in America changed the attitude of Irish-Americans from various parts of the country as they rapidly discovered each other and formed the habit of traveling over long distances. Events in Ireland and Fenian organizational efforts intensified their sense of identity as Irishmen, and in the immediate aftermath of the war the ex-peasants successfully functioned as an interest group in the halls of Congress, in the White House, and in the State Department.

In such an atmosphere the Irish naturally sought to create national organizations for other reasons. In 1869 the numerous local benevolent societies joined together to form the Irish Catholic Benevolent Union. Three years later the Catholic Total Abstinence Union held its convention in Philadelphia, with representatives of over 207 societies present. Although the Ancient Order of Hibernians claims a founding date of 1836 and an incorporation date of 1853, it did not really start to grow as a truly national organization until after the Civil War, and not until the 1890's did it surpass the power of the Irish Catholic Benevolent Union.

The history of the ICBU reveals many features of what happened to the Irish in the thirty years from 1870 to 1900. In these years, for instance, Irish and Catholic remained literally synonymous, and therefore, when Judge Dennis Dwyer formed the ICBU in 1869, he opened the organization to all Catholic societies. The Catholic Beneficial Society of Richmond, Virginia, a member of the Catholic Benevolent Union of Virginia, quite naturally joined the ICBU. No one seemed particularly concerned with the shift from Catholic at the state level to Irish-Catholic at the national level although many non-Irish Catholics served in the Richmond Society. An Italian-American by the name of Pizzini, for instance, at one time served as its president.

The link with Virginia's Catholics had a profound effect upon the national organization, for in 1873, a Virginia delegate to the national convention, Anthony M. Keiley, won the presidency and annual reelection until 1885. In a sense, he shaped the union's development.

Keiley's term in office began in the midst of a serious controversy which again reflected the problems of the Irish in these years. At the 1873 convention, Father David Phelan, editor of the Saint Louis *Western Watchman*, introduced a resolution attacking public schools as godless institutions that had contributed to the public immorality of the nation—an obvious reference to the scandals of the Grant administration. In the debate that followed few delegates disagreed, but Keiley, at the time mayor of Richmond and ex officio president of the Richmond School Board, declared that he would not vote for the resolution "because he could not cast a slur on the generous community which, although Protestant, had chosen a Catholic to be their Chief Magistrate and the head of the public schools." That statement started a four-year battle within the union and projected Keiley into national prominence. At the same time, it revealed the impact of political mobility upon Irish-Americans. What they said in the 1840's by way of condemning American institutions such as the public schools they could not say in the 1870's since they had become part of those institutions.

During his term in office Keiley shared the leadership of the union with Martin I. J. Griffin, its long-time secretary. Griffin ran the national office from Philadelphia where he also edited and published the *ICBU Journal*, the official organ of the union. Both men wanted the organization to help the Irish make a better life for themselves in the United States and concentrated their efforts on economic issues and on gaining political power. At one time they embarked upon an ambitious plan to colonize the Irish in rural Virginia. With the union's support and Keiley's personal interest, a number of Irish immigrants settled on a farm in 1877 and started to build a community they named Keileyville. In spite of this interest, however, dissension, in the Irish tradition, quickly arose, and the experiment failed.

This failure of a large-scale effort in the economic life of the immigrants only stimulated Keiley's and Griffin's interest in politics as a vehicle for the advancement of the Irish. As long as the Republicans remained in office, however, they could accomplish little. Keiley, for instance, attempted to pressure President Rutherford B. Hayes into establishing a number of Catholic chaplaincies in various homes for veterans of the Civil War, but nothing happened. Thus, the union's influence in Washington remained slight until the campaign and Democratic victory of Grover Cleveland in 1884. The new president rewarded the work of the union with a number of major appointments, including Keiley's appointment as minister to Rome. In the next few years the Irish Catholic Benevolent Union maintained its contacts in Washington under a new president, Michael Glennon. A resident of Norfolk, Virginia, he had accepted the postmaster's position there from the Cleveland administration in 1885. In the campaign of 1888 Glennon, of course, campaigned for Cleveland and, at the same time, in a little known incident, proved the power of the union in the halls of Congress.

From the end of the Civil War the Irish Catholic Benevolent Union had supported the claim for compensation by a parish priest for the Union army's destruction of a small chapel. The troops reportedly needed firewood, and the chapel filled their needs. The ICBU's attempts to have the case heard failed until the leadership brought the issue to the United States Senate in the midst of the 1888 presidential campaign. With the significance of the Catholic vote on everyone's mind, the Senate passed a special resolution to recognize the claim. The priest received his money.

The Republican victory in 1888 caused the union to lose its influence in Washington, something it never regained due to internal dissension. Keiley had, of course, left office in 1885, and Glennon proved incapable of filling his shoes. Then in the early 1890's Griffin publicly endorsed the temperance issue and quickly divided the organization on that issue. When he openly broke with the organization in 1894, the union, under new leadership, quickly lost its influence even in Catholic circles. Although in theory it continued as a national body until 1913, in practice the Ancient Order of Hibernians became the voice of the Irish in America.[3]

If the 1870's marked the emergence of such organizations as the ICBU, these years also saw other changes in the economic life of the Irish. When the immigrants first arrived, whether before or after the Civil War, they had to work at the bottom of the economic scale. Thus, we find Irish laborers working on the Erie Barge Canal in the 1820's and in the great railroad building gangs that linked one end of

America to the other in 1869. Yet at the same time many Irish-Americans from the early migrations and their children found better positions in America's economic life. Before the Civil War, for instance, the Irish made great fun of their role as volunteer firemen with each Irish ghetto sporting its share of such companies. By the end of the war, however, the concept of the volunteer fireman had waned, and paid companies appeared in the major cities. Because so many Irishmen had served in the volunteer system and because they could look forward only to jobs at the bottom of the economic scale, large numbers of them joined these new departments, and many rapidly reached positions of responsibility. These companies offered them security and economic stability the outside world could not provide. The uniforms gave them a sense of respectability; their work, a sense of accomplishment. All of these values blended with the tenets of their Catholicism and their desire to overcome the evil heritage of a dispossessed past.

For those very same reasons the Irish gravitated toward the police force in the large cities. The modern police department started to emerge only in the late 1840's and early 1850's when the post-famine Irish arrived in such large numbers. The newcomers quickly joined these departments, and in the decade that preceded the Civil War a few rose to positions of responsibility. When the riots occurred in New York in 1863, for instance, John A. Kennedy led the city's police force, and in the 1870's Thomas F. Byrnes earned a national reputation as New York's leading detective. Michael Kerwin, a Civil War veteran and Fenian conspirator, became a police commissioner in New York, while the Irish served as the major source of recruits for the force in New Orleans as well as in San Francisco.[4]

While some thus found respectability in these fields that represented law and order, other Irishmen found the same sense of position in America's unions. The labor movement had emerged from a state of infancy in the late 1840's, just as the bulk of the Irish arrived in America. Few, if any, of these peasants had had any serious experience in labor affairs, but their economic position within the country forced them into numerous labor associations. Soon the Irish skill for organization helped to form unions from New York to San Francisco, including skilled craftsmen, from tailors to bricklayers, from shoemakers to carpenters, from longshoremen to laborers and unskilled workers. At first, these unions operated on the local level, but in the 1860's the tendency toward national bodies appeared. In 1861 Martin Burke helped to form the American Miner's Association. Eighteen years later second-generation Terence V. Powderly gained control of the first truly effective national labor union, the Knights of Labor. Numerous other first- and second-generation Irish-Americans organized labor unions at the local level, many of which gradually achieved national prominence. Significantly, an Irish-American named Peter J. McGuire helped form the American Federation of Labor in 1886, but he is best remembered as the "Father of Labor Day."[5]

Americans viewed these developments as positive contributions to the labor movement, but the Irish made some negative contributions as well. In this regard, the greatest mark against them occurred in the coal fields of Pennsylvania with the formation of the Molly Maguires.

The story of the Mollies, like that of the ICBU, carried in it many of the strains that ran through the lives of Irishmen in America. It clearly shows that although by 1870 some of the Irish had reached some respectability in American society, many Irishmen remained at the bottom of the economic ladder. A large number of them still worked as laborers. The role played by the Mollies also shows the relationship of Ireland's history to the American experience, as well as the close link between the Irishman and the Catholic church. Finally, it shows what organization did for the Irish in America.

Although the public disclosures did not come until the middle of the 1870's, the story of the Molly Maguires began in Ireland, where both history and personal experience had taught the peasants that the only path to survival in a world created by absentee landlordism and British law was to take matters into one's own hands. The secret societies that flourished in bad times solved the peasants' economic and political problems, and the memory of that technique did not disappear from the minds of the famine Irish when they crossed the Atlantic.

Thousands of these people moved from the port cities of America to the coal fields of Pennsylvania and found conditions that strikingly resembled conditions in the land they had left. Immigrants from England and Wales who had arrived in America ten and twenty years before the Irish held the skilled positions in the fields, and the newcomers had to take the unskilled jobs. They had to push the coal carts in the tunnels and lift the black rocks to the surface where their children could find work for paltry sums as pickers and sorters. The high-spirited Irish Catholic with the strong back was especially galled when he had to accept work as a laborer under a skilled English Protestant miner. More often than not the majority were assigned to that kind of work; in some places a skilled miner had as many as five laborers picking up the coal he had just cut from the tunnel walls.

At first the small-town atmosphere of the coal fields re-created the sense of security that the immigrants had known in rural Ireland, but those same small towns quickly created other problems. The mine operators literally owned the towns. The immigrant lived in a company home, for which he paid rent, and bought at the company store, where most of the time he offered company script for his food. Even where the immigrant could live beyond this kind of company control, he found housing and the local storekeeper's prices beyond his means. An industry whose economic health fluctuated widely in the 1860's and 1870's and the existence of large-scale labor organizations that wanted to prove their worth produced conditions that gave the Irishman cause for complaints. He recalled the stories of Molly activities in Ireland during the 1840's and quite naturally turned to that example as the solution for his problems in America.

The first rumors that a secret society of Roman Catholics, the Molly Maguires, operated in Schuylkill County circulated among the authorities in the 1850's as the Know-Nothing movement capitalized on the anti-Catholicism of many Americans. Then in the early 1860's the Civil War increased these rumors. The Irish workers in Schuylkill County opposed the war and refused to cooperate with state officials when Pennsylvania established a draft system in 1862. The opposition grew so strong that open defiance occurred when a group of miners stopped a train loaded with recruits and told the draftees that, if they did not want to go to war, they would receive local protection from the draft law. The local draft commissioner informed Harrisburg that he could not enforce the law without a full-scale conflict with the Molly Maguires. The seriousness of the situation forced the Catholic bishop of Philadelphia, Frederick Wood, and the spiritual leader of Schuylkill County's Irishmen, to travel to the scene of the disturbance in Cass township and urge his people to comply with the law.

His appearance and the Irish acceptance of his plea foreshadowed what was to happen in New York in the following year when Archbishop Hughes had to interfere in the draft riots that followed the attempt to comply with the first national draft law. Unfortunately for the authorities in Schuylkill County, conditions in 1863 made it impossible for them to enforce the new federal law. The local draft director feared open warfare if he attempted to draft anyone against his will. Rumors told him the resisters were adequately armed with small arms and even some artillery pieces. The authorities quite simply ignored the law. They juggled figures to show that the volunteer rate was so high that the county could meet its quota of men without resorting to the draft.

Opposition to the draft thus tended to strengthen those elements among the Irish who opposed authority on principle. This was a repetition of previous experiences in Ireland. Possibly because of their success in the antidraft struggle they decided to take other matters into their own hands. A number of acts of violence, including an occasional murder, followed during the winter of 1863-64. As the rumors persisted that a secret society of Catholics committed these crimes, Bishop Wood decided to intervene for a second time. In June, 1864, he issued a pastoral letter in which he condemned all secret societies, not only the Masons and Odd Fellows, but also the Fenian Brotherhood, the Molly Maguires, the Buckshots, and others.

The average Irishman, then as now, followed the leadership of the priest in many respects, but a sizable number, then as now, resented any attempt of the priest to enter politics on the side of the opposition. What happened in Schuylkill County in the immediate aftermath of the Civil War would indicate that Bishop Wood's letter fell upon deaf ears. The number of unsolved murders increased until in 1867 forty-six such crimes remained on the books. Nine superintendents were shot in broad daylight. Such acts captured the attention of the state, even of the nation, as the New York press devoted a great deal of space to violence in the coal fields. The intensity of the interest forced the Pennsylvania state legislature to pass a Court, Police and Jail Act in 1867 which increased the forces of law and order in Schuylkill County. The number of crimes in the county fell in the following year, but the rumor that a secret society existed to right the wrongs of the miners persisted.

Life in the Pennsylvania fields became more complicated after the Civil War since it ended the relative economic prosperity the war had brought. By 1867 overproduction had glutted the market, and when one mine operator attempted to cut prices the miners went out on strike. Soon a new union appeared in the fields, the Workingmen's Benevolent Association of Saint Clair. After organizing the miners, the new union attempted to solve overproduction by suspending work. This novel approach by union men succeeded to some extent because the owners were proud individuals who acted without regard to each other. That lack of unity, however, ceased when Franklin B. Gowan, the son of an Episcopalian Irish immigrant, gained the presidency of the Reading Railroad in the spring of 1869. For the next four years the new president fought to increase his control over the coal fields by using his power to transport the coal to Philadelphia and from there to the world. Bitter battles erupted between the union and this imposing figure who wished to rule the fields.

By 1873 Gowan came to the realization that he could not control the fields until he broke the power of the Molly Maguires, who had used violence, terror, and murder to defy Gowan and the law. To accomplish this he hired the Pinkerton National Detective Agency. Fortunately, James McParlan was a logical choice for the assignment. He was born in Ulster, had worked for the agency for two years, and had an excellent knowledge of Ireland's secret societies. Under the alias of James McKenna, he arrived in the coal fields in late October, 1873. Six months later he had infiltrated the Shenandoah lodge of the Ancient Order of Hibernians.

For two and a half years McParlan collected evidence against the Molly Maguires, which he quickly discovered comprised the inner circle of the Ancient Order of Hibernians in Schuylkill County, that is, the leaders in each lodge and the county officers. These men solved their problems by ordering individuals to be beaten or murdered. Neither Allan Pinkerton nor Gowan could use this evidence, however, for fear of a premature disclosure of McParlan's true identity. Meanwhile, Gowan continued his efforts to gain total control of the fields by purchasing various mines under false registration and by eliminating competition in carrying coal to the sea. Then the financial panic of 1873 disrupted the economy and destroyed what prosperity existed in the coal fields. As conditions worsened in 1874, Gowan and the operators decided that they had to cut wages, and then offered this solution to the union in December. The miners went on strike in January, 1875. The operators under Gowan's leadership refused to discuss the issue and slowly broke the strike. By June the union was dead, and the men went back to work.

In the midst of these events, the Schuylkill County AOH faced a number of crises. Internal differencies led to a number of violent acts, including the murder of a Mahanoy City policeman, while other acts of violence were directed against mine owners. Meanwhile, McParlan diligently collected evidence and, unfortunately, found himself so enmeshed in the organization that he had to participate in the planning of murders. Then, in early September, 1875, the Mollies killed three men in broad daylight, two of them mine bosses.

These last murders inspired widespread public opposition to the Mollies and a new spirit of vigilantism spread through the coal fields. Allan Pinkerton even advised that his agents should exploit this feeling to form committees to "take fearful revenge on the Molly Maguires." The authorities quickly arrested three Irishmen for one of the September murders. Before that, a band of men had invaded the home of Charles and Ellen McAllister in Wiggans Patch and had killed Ellen McAllister, Charles O'Donnell, and James McAllister.

The Wiggans Patch massacre aroused Bishop Wood to issue a new condemnation of the Molly Maguires, "otherwise [known as] the Ancient Order of Hibernians." The trial of the September murder opened in January, 1876. Evidence disclosed there led to other arrests, and the leadership realized they had a spy in their midst. Fortunately, McParlan fled to safety in early March, and in April the papers published what they claimed were detailed confessions of murder and violence. In May, McParlan took the stand in one of the cases, and the entire Molly Maguire leadership realized that the end was near. The trials continued for the next twelve months, and in June, 1877, the state executed ten men; John Kehoe was not executed until December 18, 1878.

The incredible story, with its economic, ethnic, religious, and social overtones, profoundly influenced the image of the Irish in America. It took years for the Ancient Order of Hibernians to live down the crises, and many Americans used the incident to keep the flames of anti-Catholicism alive into the twentieth century. The whole affair is a perfect example of how life in Ireland continued to condition the thinking of those who found their way across the Atlantic.[6]

If in the minds of native Americans the Mollies created an image of wild Irish criminals, that image did not interfere with the continued movement of the Irish into the upper ranks of American society. Irishmen, for instance, began to appear in the business world. A number of them made money in the contracting business in New York and other cities, while some entered the dry-goods or department-store world. William Grace rapidly progressed toward becoming a genuine business tycoon. Irish bankers were successful in Milwaukee, San Francisco, Washington, and New York.

While many acquired wealth in a normal business way, some became wealthy overnight. An Irishman, for instance, led the party that discovered the famous Comstock silver lode, and for a generation the Irish maintained a significant community in Nevada. Others developed oil refineries and public utilities. Martin Maloney, for instance, helped organize the United Gas Improvement Company in Philadelphia in 1882.

Irish-Americans made some significant contributions to America's growing list of inventions. Michael Cudahy, for example, built his meat-packing company through a series of innovations, and John P. Holland, who perfected his submarine during the 1870's, eventually provided the United States Navy with its first operational submarine, the U.S.S. *Holland*.[7]

Irishmen appeared in the medical profession, in the sciences, and in education, and distinguished themselves in the legal world. By 1870 Charles O'Connor had a nationwide reputation. In that decade Patrick J. McCarthy, a protégé of Charles Eliot Norton, entered Harvard Law School, while another graduate of that institution, Patrick Collins, had already started to develop his reputation.[8]

II *Growing Political Power*

Of all these accomplishments and signs that individual Irishmen had arrived in American society, the greatest indication of how far the group had climbed appeared in the world of politics. During the 1870's, Hugh McLaughlin gained control of the Democratic party machine in Brooklyn and ruled it for thirty years with a few mishaps. In 1876 an influential member of the Irish Catholic Benevolent Union, Michael Jennings, won a seat on the City Council of Philadelphia, and six years later William F. Harrity, an early graduate of La Salle College, became chairman of the Philadelphia Democratic City Committee. Harrity later served as the chairman of the National Democratic Committee during

Cleveland's 1892 campaign. At least eight men, all prominent in the ICBU, held judgeships during the 1870's, and in 1880 Dennis Dwyer, founder of the union, won a seat on the New York State Supreme Court. During the 1870's, Irish-Americans served as mayors in Richmond, Memphis, Baltimore, Wilmington, and Scranton, and in 1880 William C. Grace won a bitter, bigot-ridden campaign for the mayor's job in New York. This growing political influence was not limited to local politics, for in 1871 William R. Roberts, a prominent Fenian, entered Congress as a Democratic representative from New York. In the election of 1876 James B. Reilly won a congressional seat in Pennsylvania, and in 1879 three additional Irish-Americans entered Congress as Democrats.

However, the Democrats did not have an absolute monopoly among Irish-American politicians. As early as 1868 a second-generation Irishman, Alexander Sullivan, who later became a dominant figure in radical Irish-American circles, actively campaigned for Grant's election. In return for his services, he became collector of internal revenue at Santa Fe. In 1876 William J. Sewell of Camden, New Jersey, served as a delegate to the National Republican Convention and later represented that state in the United States Senate. William Woodburn of Nevada was a Republican congressman from 1875 to 1877, and two other Republican Irishmen entered the House in 1879. Senator Simon B. Conover, a Republican from Florida, served as an active member of the Clan-na-Gael, the leading radical organization in America. During the 1880's four Republicans and eleven Democrats Irish-Americans served in the House, while three served in the Senate. Some had actively participated in the Fenian movement in the 1860's. [9]

The career of Patrick Collins clearly reflects Irish-American influence on American politics. Even as he was actively engaged in organizing the Fenians at the end of the Civil War, he won a seat in the Massachusetts General Court. Three years later, in 1870, he moved to the State Senate and in 1873 became Democratic city chairman in Boston. This led to his appointment as the State's judge advocate-general and to the Democratic National Committee. In the state elections of 1876 the Democrats of Massachusetts reaped the benefits. In that year, Charles Francis Adams carried the Democratic banner in his fight for the governorship of Massachusetts, but Irish-Americans were displeased with him for his record as minister to England during and after the Civil War. They accused him of refusing to defend Irish-born American citizens arrested by the British on charges of inciting the Irish population to revolt. Collins himself made such accusations in 1867, but in 1876 he publicly reversed his position and defended Adams' record. Collins' biographer claimed that his intervention saved at least thirteen thousand votes for the Democrats. Four years later Collins served as a delegate to the National Convention and ran for Congress. His election made him a power at the national level of the Democratic party for twenty years.[10]

This kind of individual success for Irish-Americans appeared in various parts of the country in the 1870's, but the Irish gained their greatest political power in New York City when they won control of Tammany Hall. They controlled it with absolute authority for fifty years.

The Irish did not always belong to Tammany. William Mooney formed the Society of Tammany in 1789 as a social and benevolent society, but Aaron Burr quickly saw the political potential of the new organization. He infiltrated the leadership with his own men and used the society to organize the campaign of 1800, which delivered New York City to Thomas Jefferson. Aaron Burr led a Society that sought the votes of the working class, but that fourth-generation Puritan and grandson of Jonathan Edwards, would not permit the Irish to enter the society itself. Not until 1809 did Tammany permit Irish Catholics on its ticket, when Patrick McKay ran for the Assembly, but the prejudice continued, and on April 24, 1817 the Irish marched to Tammany Hall to urge the chiefs to nominate Thomas Addis Emmet, an Irish patriot of 1798, for Congress.

This tendency of Tammany to remain anti-foreign and 100 percent American, however, did not last forever. In the immediate aftermath of the Napoleonic Wars, immigration from Ireland increased, and the Irish population in New York grew. At the same time, Tammany fought for universal manhood suffrage mainly because only in this way could the chiefs break the political control of the wealthy classes in New York. They gained their objective when the Constitution of 1821 granted every white man in the state the right to vote. Coupled with the lack of a secret ballot system for voting, this constitutional change gave Tammany the power to control elections in the city. Once in office, a Tammany man would then take what he could from tax receipts and use these funds to guarantee his reelection.

In this atmosphere of corruption, the spoils system, and the influx of foreigners who had to be naturalized rapidly (legally or illegally), control of Tammany fell into the hands of Martin Van Buren, who used his experience to create a machine which won the presidency for Jackson in 1828. Although he used the rising Irish voters in that election, Van Buren and the other Tammany leaders soon discovered that they had to give more places to newcomers. In the 1830's the Irish used their saloons as neighborhood political headquarters, and they used roving bands of toughs to guarantee their power at the polls under such colorful leaders as Mike Walsh, editor of *Subterranean*. In the 1840's, however, power in Tammany shifted from Van Buren to a new figure who had a great following among the Irish, but who remained truly an American, Fernando Wood.

To a great extent, Wood's rule of Tammany, which became absolute in the 1850's, served as the start of the transition period for the city and the Irish. Prior to this arrival at the helm, the Irish remained on the fringe of power in New York City, but the great migrations of the late 1840's and early 1850's gave them political control of the city. In 1850, 117,000 Irishmen arrived in the city and over 100,000 came in the following year. This enormous ethnic concentration gave Wood the political leverage to create an absolute monarchy for himself in Tammany, and after some bitter clashes with the Know-Nothings, he emerged as mayor of New York in January, 1855.

Wood's first term surprised everyone who expected that he would ignore the need for reforms and hand the city over to his Tammany lieutenants. In a number of sweeping reform moves, he earned the title of the "Model Mayor," but his morality did not extend to elections. In his second campaign he used all the old techniques of driving his opponents from the polls by using roving Irish gangs and by stuffing the ballot boxes. When he emerged victorious for a second time, he again shifted his position and opened the city to the old corruption. Land was sold to the city for exorbitant sums, and Mayor Wood sold offices at will.

In these years of Wood's rule two Irishmen appeared among the men of Tammany's lower ranks, William Tweed and "Honest John" Kelly. Both would later rule the Hall and the city for twenty years, complete the transition to Irish rule, and establish the base for its continuation well into the twentieth century.

Bill Tweed's father had emigrated from Ireland in the aftermath of the Napoleonic Wars and quickly developed a successful business in New York. At an early age Bill spent his time at the head of a local gang. After he married, his father paved the way for him to lead the life of a successful businessman, but he preferred to join a volunteer fire company. There he used his enormous size to fight opposing companies. From these street brawls he moved quickly into politics. From the Seventh Ward, which changed from a middle-class district to an immigrant area in the 1840's, Tweed entered City Council on the Tammany ticket and quickly learned how to make money. During the 1850's, however, he found his greatest obstacle to success in the person of Fernando Wood, and he quickly formed an alliance with Peter Sweeney, Dick Connally, and George Barnard to exile Wood from the city. They accomplished this in 1862 when Wood agreed to go to Congress, and Tweed gained absolute control of Tammany.

For the next seven years "Boss" Tweed milked the city dry. In a number of amazing moves he placed his friends in all the important offices and arranged for judges to naturalize future Democrats at the rate of hundreds a day. In 1868, for instance, a total of 41,112 immigrants took the oath as United States citizens. With these voters he manipulated elections at will, and when he could not find real voters he manufactured them. In the five years that followed the Civil War he and his gang took millions in tax receipts and sold legislation from his position as a state senator in Albany. To guarantee his ability to control the city, he had the legislature pass a new city charter, which conveniently created government bodies that he personally controlled. Tammany could steal with assurance of absolute safety. He had to pay some rural legislators as much as $20,000 apiece to get this new charter passed, but it was a solid investment. By 1870 Tweed had all the appurtenances of wealth—large homes, estates, yachts, horses, and so on—and he could truthfully say he owned Tammany, city hall, the state legislature, two thirds of the State Supreme Court, and the governor's mansion in Albany.

All this exploded in the summer of 1871 when dissension split the happy family; Sheriff Jimmy O'Brien gave the New York *Times* evidence that Tweed's gang had defrauded the city. The disclosures quickly led to arrests. The court convicted Tweed on 104 separate counts of crime. Charles O'Connor, the brilliant Irish lawyer, prosecuted the case, and "Honest John" Kelly took Tweed's place as ruler of Tammany and the city.

John Kelly was born in 1822. His father owned a grocery store, but he died when John was eight. The young boy then left the parochial school to care for his typically Irish-Catholic mother. Although at first he thought of the priesthood, he gradually gravitated to politics, and his election in the Sixth Ward in 1853 marked the emergence of the Irish in that district. Two years later he won a seat in Congress, where, as the only Roman Catholic present, he bitterly defended his people against the attacks of the Know-Nothings. He became a force in Tammany politics and nominated Wood for his second term in 1856. Then he resigned from Congress and successfully ran for the office of sheriff of New York county. There he remained for six years and amassed a small fortune "honestly and fairly." Then personal tragedy struck, with the death of his wife and a son. He withdrew from New York, traveled to Europe and the Holy Land, and returned at the height of the Tweed Ring scandals.

The situation in New York demanded reform of Tammany, and Kelly decided he would lead the fight. After a bitter struggle he defeated the "Gang" and replaced them with men of high stature in the city. Yet Horatio Seymour, August Belmont, Abram Hewitt, and the others knew that something important had happened. Tweed may have been born of a father who came from Ireland, but his grandfather had emigrated from Scotland. The Protestant-Irish Tweed now gave way to the Irish-Catholic Kelly. Not until 1962 would another Protestant rule Tammany Hall.

John Kelly ruled Tammany with an iron hand until his death in 1885, but he did so without the voice and bluster of previous leaders. A quiet man with an analytical mind, he decided that election victories demanded a proper organization and carefully created the basic big-city political structure that every "boss" since has copied. At the same time he created a new attitude and set rules for the political leader to use in gaining the allegiance of the people. Those rules remained without change until the New Deal of the 1930's assigned to the federal bureaucracy the task of caring for the poor. He organized the party from the block captain to the precinct captain to the ward boss, from the voters to the ward convention to the general committee. He ruled over all. He won elections by dispensing personal favors to the voters and the party workers. His victories gave him control of more public offices from which he dispensed more favors. He saw to it that the workers in the districts cared for the ignorant and bewildered immigrants. They found the immigrants jobs and gave them clothes, food, and coal in the winter. Bail money came from Tammany men, and many a Christmas turkey arrived at a voter's home with a word of thanks from Tammany. Kelly created an invisible government that cared for the needs of the people in an informal manner and made the huge city of New York warm and friendly. His power grew out of the enormous social service agency he created.

Using these methods, he marshaled the voters from the working class (Shorthairs) and then linked them to the wealthy (Swallowtails) to give Tammany power and respectability at the same time. The alliance with the rich, however, did not last, and in 1876 Kelly split with Samuel Tilden, a prominent Swallowtail who wanted the Democratic presidential nomination. Kelly agreed to support Tilden if he won the nomination, and in November, 1876, Manhattan gave the Democratic candidate enough votes to offset the Republican majority in upstate New York. Yet the split with Kelly caused the Swallowtails to form a new organization, "Irving Hall," which in turn led to a bitter battle in the 1878 Democratic State Convention. When the party nominated a Tilden man for governor, Kelly stalked out of the convention, declaring himself a candidate for the governorship, and proceeded to split the Democratic vote, thus giving the victory to the Republican, Alonzo Cornell. Two years later Kelly agreed to unite behind the Democratic candidate for president, but he also pledged his support to William Grace for mayor, thus raising the Catholic issue in the city. The Democrats lost the state because the Democratic city votes did not offset the upstate Republican lead. The unwillingness to support the party's nominee forced many upstate Democrats to split with Kelly, and, in 1882, it became evident in the Democratic State Convention when the party nominated Grover Cleveland for governor. The new governor refused Kelly's request for patronage and condemned a Tammany attempt to block his appointments. The bitterness of the dispute led to a Kelly attempt to kill Cleveland's chance for the Democratic presidential nomination in 1884. He failed, of course, but the Irish influence in the campaign was substantial. Kelly died shortly after the election, and Richard Croker, another Irish-Catholic, gained control of Tammany. Kelly may not have had enough power to select the candidates for all national offices, but he certainly had proven that the Irish in New York could no longer be ignored.[11]

The events of the 1870's displayed the Irish rise to a position of power in many parts of American society, and many Americans took note of it. They agreed with the words of Robert Ellis Thompson in 1880, then professor of political economy at the University of Pennsylvania and in 1883 the first dean of the famed Wharton School: "We have the Irishman, excitable, over-imaginative, improvident, as it is generally thought, but given free play in business and public affairs, it cannot be denied that his political achievements among us, whatever else may be said of them, have shown great adroitness and method; and the Celt in the county also makes money, builds up fortunes."[12]

CHAPTER 6

Years of Preparation

I *Elements of Irish Power*

THE rising influence of the Irish in America not only affected Americans; it also changed the character of the centuries-old Anglo-Irish struggle. Whereas the British fought a national movement in the 1840's, they faced an international problem in the 1880's. Ireland was no longer poor. No longer did she stand without powerful allies.[1] The immigrants in America could send money to Ireland and simultaneously force the United States to intervene in the Anglo-Irish struggles. They could do so because of a series of events that occurred toward the end of the 1870's and at the start of the 1880's.

It was fortunate for Ireland, that while the ex-peasants gained a measure of political power, material affluence, and social position in America, they did not forget their heritage. They passed sordid tales of English oppression to the next generation in the form of family legends. The fact that their parents had been "frozen out" by the despised British landlords created in the later generations "an affection for Ireland as ardent as the most national[istic] native-born inhabitant of Cork, the very capital of Irish nationality." British travelers recognized this "deep feeling of resentment against England."

The numerous and now nationally organized Irish societies helped to keep these sentiments alive, and in the late 1870's a thriving Irish-American press fanned these flames ever higher. In 1870 Patrick Ford founded the New York *Irish World*, which eventually became the most influential radical Irish paper in America and possibly even in Ireland. By 1880 four additional Irish papers were published in New York, and every important center of Irish population supported at least one newspaper. In 1876 John Boyle O'Reilly became the proprietor as well as editor of the Boston *Pilot*, which he made into the leading organ of conservative

[75]

Irish-American nationalism. In 1882 John F. Finerty established the Chicago *Citizen*, another important radical sheet, while the *Western Watchman* appeared in Saint Louis, the *Northwestern Chronicle* in Saint Paul, and the *Irish Catholic Benevolent Union Journal* in Philadelphia. By 1880 they were the "principal instrument of instruction in Irish-American nationalism."[2] Neither the immigrant nor his children could forget the past. With the old sentiments alive and the tools to intensify them readily available, the Irish in America waited for an opportunity to use their power. Certain changes then occurred in Irish and Irish-American nationalism, American politics, and Anglo-American relations that would quickly converge to give them that chance.

By 1875 it became clear to all that the Irish nationalist movement in America needed reorganization. The revolutionary element that had dominated the Irish in America from 1848 to 1870 lost control of Irish political aspirations after the Fenian fiascos to a more moderate faction which emphasized the constitutional, parliamentary approach to the solution of the Irish Question. Men like John Boyle O'Reilly and Patrick Collins, both of Boston, Thomas Meehan of New York, and Anthony M. Keiley of Richmond, Virginia, emerged as the leaders of the latter group. Both O'Reilly and Collins had actively participated in the 1866-67 revolution, O'Reilly as an organizer in the British army, and Collins as an organizer in the United States, but the failure of the revolt caused them to lose confidence in the use of physical force. O'Reilly withdrew from the Irish Revolutionary Brotherhood in 1870 and welcomed the Home Rule party when it emerged four years later in Ireland. Collins, meanwhile, settled in Boston where he entered upon his career in American politics. Both men had received wide recognition of their roles as leaders of this more conservative movement. Keiley had condemned the Fenians in 1866, yet emerged as president of the Irish Catholic Benevolent Union in 1873 and from that position led the organization into the purely American ventures described above. All three remained intensely loyal to the Democratic party.

The prominence of these men, however, did not mean the elimination of more radical elements. The decline of the Fenians was offset somewhat by the formation of a separate organization for hard-core revolutionaries within the IRB. Founded in 1867, this new group, the Clan-na-Gael, slowly developed as the dominant "physical force power in Irish-American nationalism." By 1876 it numbered over 1,000 members and controlled sufficient wealth to think in terms of armed attacks upon English cities. In addition, by the end of the decade Patrick Ford and O'Donovan Rossa had collected special funds for direct and violent attacks upon the hated English. The radicals, in effect, had reemerged to struggle for the leadership of the Irish in America.[3]

While these changes occurred in America, nationalism in Ireland experienced a similar change. After the failure of O'Connell, the Irish people wandered across the political stage without an effective leader. Neither the Young Irelanders nor the Irish Revolutionary Brotherhood produced a voice capable of capturing the imagination of the Irish nation as a whole, or of dominating Parliament for the good of Ireland. Then in 1875 a rather obscure Protestant descendant of the Anglo-Irish Ascendancy, Charles Stewart Parnell, won his first seat in the House of Commons as a Home Ruler. Within two years he had emerged as the leader of a small group within the party, the "obstructionists." A new light appeared. Ireland found a dynamic leader capable of simultaneously capturing Ireland's masses and disrupting the quiet calm of the House of Commons.

While Parnell slowly emerged as the dominant Irish parliamentarian, other Irish nationalists in both Ireland and America began another drive to destroy England's control of Ireland. In August, 1877, J. J. O'Kelly suggested that some means of uniting the many facets of Irish and Irish-American nationalism would have to be found if Ireland were ever to be free. In the following June John Boyle O'Reilly, the Irish-born Boston politician, suggested the calling of a national convention to unite all shades of Irish opinion. Then, in August, 1878, Michael Davitt, an Irish agricultural reformer, came to America to visit his mother, and the Clan-na-Gael organized a lecture tour for him.

That tour ended in a merging of the agitation for land reform in Ireland, the growing Irish parliamentary movement, and the various factions in America under what the participants called the New Departure. Devoy, Ford, and O'Reilly joined hands. In March, 1879, Devoy met Parnell in Paris. Both agreed in general terms that the new movement, although basically agrarian, would establish a national public organization in which the extremists as well as the moderates would have an opportunity to arouse public opinion. A strange union of forces emerged—one that eventually rocked the very foundations of the Anglo-Irish Ascendancy.[4] Oddly enough, however, the real strength of the new effort rested upon forces beyond anyone's control.

Although the Irish land system that operated during the 1870's represented an improvement over the situation in the late 1840's, it still had many defects. Over 90 percent of the people occupied small holdings without right of tenure, except that based upon the payment of rent, and made their living from the land. Many still depended upon the potato for sustenance and paid their rent with profits from a money crop or—between the planting and harvesting of the potato—by traveling to England to work as laborers in the agriculture industry. If catastrophe struck either side of this dual economy, the peasant usually faced an unpleasant winter. If it struck the potato, he faced the choice of starvation unless he used his rent money to purchase food for his family. But if he did, eviction was certain. His situation would be bad enough if only the potato failed; but if agricultural prices fell at the same time, the peasant faced an utterly hopeless future. He could neither eat nor pay.[5]

The partial failure of the potato crop in 1878 and the falling prices of other crops threatened a recurrence of the pattern of the 1840's and 1850's. The total value of all Irish crops fell from about £36,000,000 in 1876 to about £22,000,000 in 1879, an enormous loss of 38 percent in itself, but the more startling when one considers that the potato crop's value alone fell from £12,464,000 to only £3,341,000, a 75 percent decrease.

In the midst of the unrest which this economic loss created in the spring of 1879, Davitt organized the Mayo Land League. On June 5, 1879, Parnell addressed this body at Westport. By midsummer, Davitt, riding the tide of unrest, organized branches throughout the country and finally changed the league's name by dropping "Mayo" and adding "National." In October Parnell accepted the presidency of the National Land League and the leadership of a growing wave of agrarian agitation. He also promised to travel to America to seek the necessary funds and to establish permanent branches of the league.[6] America stood on the edge of a decade of involvement with Ireland.

At this critical juncture when the decaying economic situation in Ireland strengthened Davitt's plan, American politics entered a relatively unique period during which the old bitter memories of

Irish-Americans were again aroused, and the groundwork was laid for Parnell's leadership during the 1880's. In 1872, in spite of numerous handicaps, Grant and the Republican party had won the White House because Democrats in the North had failed to vote and Republicans had reconstructed the South. Yet in 1874 the Democrats captured the House of Representatives for the first time in sixteen years, and they looked forward to a victory in the election of 1876. The South—all but Florida, Louisiana, and South Carolina—had already emerged from the control of carpetbaggers. Also, the nomination of Samuel J. Tilden offered the greatest opportunity to campaign against the corruption of "Grantism." The struggle, however, resulted in the closest election in history, and only a political deal gave the White House to the Republican, Rutherford B. Hayes, in exchange for a promise to end Reconstruction. A month after entering office the new president ordered federal troops out of the South.

As the troops moved out of the South, the era of Reconstruction closed, but a new period of "no-decision" opened. From 1876 to 1896 the relative strengths of the two major parties remained virtually equal as election after election turned on incredibly few votes.[7] This numerical equality created a world of static politics. Since a mere handful of voters could decide an election, the professionals ignored the problems of the times and sought victory by waving "the bloody shirt" or by attacking a candidate's private life. They avoided real issues with an obsession, for victory rested less upon one's ability to present ideas to the voters and more on one's ability to manipulate party machinery. They also avoided innovations because new programs generated ideas and forced people to take positions on issues which, in turn, would possibly cause an uncontrollable shift in voting patterns. Only if the politicians could predict the impact would they use something new. Thus, they presented to the American people only two issues—the tariff and government reform—but even on these points both major parties split evenly.[8]

In this situation of numerical equality and static politics, politicians sought issues that would attract voters from the other side without causing any shift from their own base. In their search they assumed that the Democrats could expect to win at least the 153 electoral votes of the southern and border states and the Republicans could control northern and western states for 182 electoral votes. Victory or defeat thus rested upon the results in New York, New Jersey, Indiana, and Connecticut, and both parties concentrated their resources in these states. If the Democrats won all but New York, they would fall short of victory by 18 votes. The Republicans in turn could win by taking this all-important state—provided the Democrats made no inroads into their bloc. In this way New York held a position in national politics far out of proportion to its size or population and virtually dominated presidential elections from 1880 to 1892. Fortunately, John Kelly and Richard Croker ruled Tammany, and they could speak to thousands of Irish voters.[9]

In that political climate of the 1880's, events occurred in the world of Anglo-American diplomacy that indicated the possible return of hard-core Anglophobia. In the years immediately preceding the election of Rutherford B. Hayes, Anglo-American relations remained rather peaceful and calm, the result of the Treaty of Washington, British statesmanship under Gladstone, and the wise diplomacy of Hamilton Fish. However, in 1874 Gladstone left office. Benjamin Disraeli returned and led England down the road to a new imperialism. Three years later Fish gave the keys to his office to William M. Evarts, a much less qualified and gifted statesman. In addition, the goodwill generated by the Treaty of Washington suffered a serious blow in November, 1877, with the announcement of the Halifax award. The United States owed Great Britain $5,500,000 as the monetary difference between the American use of the Canadian inshore fisheries and Canadian rights to ship duty-free fish into the American market. Americans quickly condemned the decision; Anglophobia had returned to the surface of American life.

Before the effect of this decision wore off, the Fortune Bay incident occurred. In January, 1878, an angry mob of British citizens drove a group of American fishermen from the Canadian shore and damaged American property. Evarts protested the incident and demanded an investigation by the British. After an exchange of notes, he eventually claimed over $100,000 in damages and asked the British to settle the question as soon as possible. The British refused to accept the American claim, and the issue remained an open sore in Anglo-American relations until the summer of 1881.

Meanwhile, the British return to a policy of active imperialism created other areas of friction. From 1875 to 1879 the United States and England struggled over control of the Samoan Islands in the South Pacific. Before the two nations had settled that problem they tangled over a dispute between Chile and Bolivia. In February, 1879 Chile started the War of the Pacific to control certain nitrate deposits. By June Americans pictured the whole thing as a British-inspired war, and many favored American action to preserve America's interests. In the midst of that preoccupation, the question of a French-built and -controlled canal across the isthmus of Panama arose. This eventually generated a movement in Congress to abrogate the Clayton-Bulwer Treaty, which had regulated American-British relations in that area of the world since 1850. Anglo-American relations received another jolt when Indians under the leadership of Sitting Bull crossed the border into the United States from Canada, swiftly returning after destroying American lives and property. Evarts demanded that British authorities prevent such attacks but received no encouragement. Under these circumstances, Anglophobia increased.[10]

As the decade of the 1870's closed, the conditions that had given the Irish so much influence at the end of the Civil War began to reappear. Once again America's politicians needed the Irish vote. America's diplomats found their negotiating position in Anglo-American quarrels strengthened by the existence of Irish-American efforts to remove the British from Ireland. At the same time, conditions in Ireland created the possibility for another attempt to overthrow British rule. In other words, just when American politicians needed Irish votes, events in Ireland intensified the ex-peasants' hatred of England and love of Ireland and unified the Irish in America around the one issue the politicians could use to win Irish support.

II *Anglo-Irish Struggle in American Politics*

The key to understanding this chance cluster of events and how it influenced the Irish in America is to be sought in what happened in Ireland. By December, 1879, the combination of falling prices for farm products in general and the 75 percent failure of the potato crop in particular caused conditions in Ireland to reach the famine stage. The threat of eviction rose considerably, and, as in past years, agrarian crime spread throughout the country. To the English, living there was like walking over a crater, "where the foulest deeds of ferocity are executed without a scruple."[11] This massive misery fostered the growth of the Land League, but both Davitt and Parnell knew that their success depended ultimately upon the Irish in America. To gain the support of that essential element, Parnell crossed the Atlantic.

The president of the Land League arrived in New York City on January 3, 1880 and in the next eleven weeks traveled as far west as Des Moines, Iowa; as far south as Richmond, Virginia; and as far north as Montreal, Canada. He spoke in forty-one cities, seventeen states; addressed legislative bodies in Virginia, Kentucky, and Iowa; and capped his tour with an invitation to address the House of Representatives. His speeches, plus the news from Ireland, aroused native Americans as well as Irish-Americans, and he managed to collect large sums for his work in Ireland. General elections forced Parnell's return to Ireland in March, but Patrick Collins, the Boston Democrat, created the American Land League in May. Parnell would continue to receive the money so necessary for his success.[12]

Parnell, meanwhile, won reelection to Parliament in the most important campaign of his life. Prior to that election, Parnell had been the leader of a small faction in the Home Rule party, but his reelection to Parliament and conditions in Ireland suddenly propelled him into the role of party leader. He had, in effect, tied the parliamentary movement to the growing misery of the peasants—and both to powerful allies in the United States. Thus, the stage was set for his assault upon English rule in Ireland.[13]

At that time, the American Irish numbered over 1.8 million with an estimated 2.7 million children. Sixty-three percent of these lived on the Atlantic coast from North Carolina to Maine. One-half million lived in New York alone, where an estimated ninety thousand of them could vote.[14]

By the spring of 1880 leaders of both major parties knew that the presidential election would be close and that victory would demand the capture of New York. They also realized that the Irish voters of that state would play a major role in the final outcome of the elections. In addition, the party bosses knew they could easily gain the attention of these voters by appealing to their interest in Ireland's freedom or to their hatred of England. Republicans, especially, eyed the Irish because of their past record of voting almost exclusively for the Democratic ticket.[15] Thus, as events in

Ireland captured American headlines and both parties maneuvered to capture New York state, political interest in the Irish showed itself early in the presidential campaign.

An Irish-American Republican convention opened in Indianapolis on July 18. There the speakers argued that the blind obedience of their fellow Irish-Americans to the Democratic party had earned them precious little. If the Irish expected the nation to cater to their needs, they would have to offer their votes to the Republicans. By early August an Irish-American Republican Association appeared in New York City, and soon others followed in Brooklyn, Buffalo, Syracuse, and as far away as Boston and Chicago. On September 27, the New York Irish Republicans held their own convention in Saratoga.

Meanwhile, the Democrats, aware of Republican inroads, publicized their concern for the Irish by granting prominent places in the party to Irish spokesmen. Patrick Collins, now president of the American Land League, attended the Democratic National Convention where he heard Daniel Dougherty, Irish Democrat from Pennsylvania, nominate Winfield S. Hancock for the presidency of the United States. Collins also received the nomination for Congress from a safe district in Boston, while John Boyle O'Reilly argued the Democratic cause in his Boston *Pilot*.

As only the more radical Irish elements drifted toward the Republican party, other Irish leaders in New York, Chicago, Saint Louis, and Richmond fought hard for the Democratic ticket. John Devoy, for instance, supported Garfield, while James Brady, an old Fenian from Virginia and a voice in the Irish Catholic Benevolent Union, took to the stump for Garfield. Thomas Bannerman, a prominent member of the Clan-na-Gael, helped to organize the Irish Republicans in New York.

However, in spite of this Republican activity, Irish voters stayed with the Democratic party, partly because they still associated Republicanism with Know-Nothingism and partly because Ireland did not begin to boil until late in the fall, but more importantly because the Republicans did not find an issue that would tie Irish interests directly to American politics early enough in the campaign to make a difference. Not until October did Republicans link the issue of tariff protection to the Irish, when they equated a vote for the free trade policies of Hancock and the Democrats with a vote for the interest of England. British free trade had ruined Ireland, and they prophesied it would ruin America.

Garfield won the critical state of New York and thus the White House, but only because Kelly's support of William R. Grace for the mayor's office had introduced the Catholic issue into the city's campaign. That meant that Kelly did not deliver a large enough majority in the city to offset the upstate Republican vote. Regardless of why that happened, the Irish had clearly shown their power to disrupt the plans of the national leadership and at the same time control New York. That lesson did not fail to influence the leaders of both parties.[16]

After the election the American Irish shifted their thoughts to Ireland. Their continued power in America clearly rested on their cohesiveness, and that sense of unity was dependent upon events in Ireland. If agitation ceased there, the Irish in America would have no issue around which to unite. Fortunately for them, Britain had failed to alleviate the conditions in Ireland during the summer of 1880, and in the fall Parnell and his Home Rulers moved through the country urging the people to unite against evictions. This led to Parnell's arrest on November 2; but agrarian crimes continued to increase, and evictions rapidly fell.

In January, Parnell went to trial in Dublin under ordinary law, but the jury freed him. William Gladstone, now prime minister, responded with a call for coercion laws that suspended ordinary rights.[17]

These events captured the imagination of the Irish in America, and money continued to flow into Ireland to support Parnell's fight against evictions. In the fall of 1880, however, Patrick Ford, the editor of the New York *Irish World*, and Patrick Collins, the Boston politician and president of the American Land League, disagreed on the question of who would send to whom the money collected by the League. Collins feared that Ford would use the money for radical activities, and Ford in turn boycotted the League's convention in Buffalo in January, 1881. One hundred and fifty delegates from two hundred branches attended, but no Ford-controlled branch was represented. Yet this division did not stop the flow of money to Ireland, as both moderates and radicals alike saw in Parnell their only immediate hope against British suppression of Irish freedom.

This somewhat unnatural alliance continued into March, 1881, but then events strained its continuation. Parliament passed new coercion laws, and Ford wanted Parnell to endorse open revolution. Parnell did not follow a course so contrary to his and Ireland's interests, however, and instead issued a series of ambiguous statements on the new laws. He hoped to maintain radical American support and not lose control of events in Ireland to the more violent voices. To insure the link with America he sent Patrick Egan, treasurer of the National Land League, to Paris. His balancing act appeared successful in the late spring. By May 1, 1881, the American Land League had sent over $100,000 to Ireland, and by June 1, the number of local branches had grown to over twelve hundred.[18] The Irish land war of 1880-81 had obviously so captured the imagination of the ex-peasants in America that disagreements within the leadership on both sides of the Atlantic did not endanger their willingness to send money to stop evictions.

The tragedy of the Irish soon influenced Americans in general. Numerous state legislatures passed resolutions condemning British actions in Ireland, and many newspapers followed a similar line. The reemergence of that traditional American feeling of Anglophobia contributed to much of the criticism that appeared in papers and magazines, but native American interest in Ireland rested ultimately upon the American tradition of helping any people who fought to establish their own government. Irish-American interests had merged with American interests, a development that tended to make the American Irish seem more American by supporting revolution in Ireland. Yet this unique turn of events ultimately depended upon what happened in Ireland and specifically upon Parnell's ability to balance the various factions that had combined to foster Irish and Irish-American nationalism. Unfortunately, he was faced with another hard test of nerves in the fall of 1881.

During the summer of 1881, Parliament passed a bill which provided fixity of rents, tenure of land, and compensation for improvements. Gladstone hoped that this would end the agitation of the peasants, but that hope seriously frightened the extremists on both sides of the Atlantic. If Gladstone's dream came true, the land war would end. The peasants would give up, and England would continue to rule Ireland. The radicals only hope lay in Parnell's issuance of a "no-rent manifesto"—a call for the nonpayment of rents and a virtual declaration of civil war. At first, Parnell refused to issue such a call, but his mild opposition to the new laws quickly led to his arrest in October and a British attempt to suppress the Land League. From his jail cell Parnell issued the call for "no-rent." He had lost control of events. The land war now raged in earnest.

The events of October unified the Irish in support of Parnell and his movement and led to a call for a great convention. Two parliamentary associates of Parnell and a priest-organizer for the National Land League traveled to Chicago to explain to the delegates what was happening at home and what they needed. Over one thousand delegates from thirty-eight states (a sharp increase over the Buffalo meeting) heard John Finerty, editor of the Chicago *Citizen*, call the convention to order and ask for a pledge of $250,000 to resist evictions. The delegates endorsed his plan, and funds soon arrived in Paris where Patrick Egan, treasurer of the National Land League, could function free of English control; Parnell remained in jail.

With this money the Ladies Land League, first organized in New York City by Parnell's sister in 1880, now attempted to fill the gap left by the suppression of the Land League.[19] The ladies moved throughout Ireland, organizing the people against evictions and the payment of rents.

By the New Year, Gladstone and his cabinet realized that their effort to rule Ireland by force had failed. By neutralizing Parnell and the Land League, Gladstone had given control of events to the extremists. Agrarian crimes rapidly increased, and evictions just as rapidly decreased in the winter of 1881-82. Captain Moonlight, a name given to the activists, and those who sympathized with the Clan-na-Gael's philosophy of physical force as the only solution for Ireland's independence had created the conditions of civil war. Twenty-five thousand troops, twenty thousand constables, and thousands of spies could not control Ireland.[20]

The chaos of these months inspired a number of Irish-Americans to enter the struggle against evictions, and their actions quickly forced the United States government into the dispute just as James G. Blaine, a professional "twister-of-the-Lion's-tail," assumed his position as secretary of state under the Republican President Garfield.

As early as the winter of 1880-81 a number of Irish-Americans returned to the "old sod" to participate in what they hoped would evolve into an open battle against England. Parliament passed the various coercion acts in early 1881, however, and British authorities quickly arrested a number of persons on mere suspicion and without right of trial by jury, including a number of American citizens. At first, both Secretary Blaine and the American minister in London, James Russell Lowell, refused to extend American protection to common criminals, but the Irish in America brought enormous pressure upon James Garfield's administration and forced Blaine by late May into a policy that demanded trial by jury for all American citizens regardless of English laws or of the nature of the crimes of the accused.

Other cases quickly came to light, and soon prominent members of Congress interceded at the White House and the State Department. As conditions in Ireland deteriorated in the summer and the autumn of 1881, more American citizens of Irish descent entered the agrarian agitation. The British responded with more arrests, and the pressures upon Blaine and Lowell increased. Both searched for a way out of a difficult situation, and, finally, in November Blaine asked the British if they would free all American citizens on the condition that they would leave the country.

By then Garfield had died, and Chester Arthur had become president. In December Frederick Frelinghuysen, who succeeded Blaine in the State Department, adopted a policy of reducing Anglo-American disagreements. The wild conditions in Ireland during the winter of 1881-82, however, kept the "American suspects" case, as it was now called, alive. Congress again became concerned, and in February New York's Representative Abram S. Hewitt introduced the question of these American suspects on the floor of the House in the midst of an appropriations bill debate. For four days Congress debated how best to protect the rights of American citizens who resided abroad; many members demanded policies the administration had no power to implement. The new secretary of state again asked the British for speedy trials for all American citizens arrested in Ireland, but he received no satisfaction. Meanwhile, the Irish organized protest meetings, while the politicians bitterly condemned the administration's handling of the case. The British minister in Washington claimed that the Irish vote had tyrannized Congress, while some American commentators felt that the power of the Irish in the cities of America exerted far too much influence on the nation's politics. In that atmosphere the British foreign minister offered to free all American "suspects" if they promised to leave Ireland—a solution to the president's problems with Congress. That offer marked British capitulation to the Irish in America and their ability to influence Congress.[21]

At the same time, England's prime minister realized that neither he nor the empire could solve the Irish problem, and he thus opened negotiations with Charles Parnell to end the agitation. On April 10 the two men reached an agreement, the Kilmainham Pact, and on May 2 Parnell left jail. His release marked the end of the land war, and relative calm returned to Ireland in the summer of 1882. Before Ambassador Lowell could assess the impact of these developments upon the "Suspects" case, he found himself facing another crisis.

On May 6 a group of extremists, the "Invincibles", murdered the newly appointed chief secretary for Ireland and his undersecretary, Thomas Burke, in Phoenix Park, Dublin, a short distance from Dublin Castle. The crime shocked Ireland, England, and America; but in dramatic fashion it raised the whole question of America's relationship with radical Irish-Americans. As early as 1877, various radical Irish-Americans called for violent attacks upon England and prepared specific plans to terrorize the British. Thus, while the peasants, Parnell, and the Land League created one set of conditions that permitted the Irish in America to use their growing political and economic power against England, the radicals in New York, Boston, and Chicago created another set of circumstances that would eventually strain Anglo-American relations to a breaking point.

In 1880-81 the radical Irish-American press published stories about various plots to destroy life and property in England. The British minister in Washington constantly complained to American officials about such articles, but neither Blaine nor Frelinghuysen indicated any willingness to act against these papers. American authorities claimed that they could not act until the Irish committed a crime on American soil.

Most Americans had no idea of radical Irish activity in America in 1880-81 since the struggles of Parnell and his Land League captured the headlines. Widespread public knowledge of radical agitation came only after the highly publicized murders of Lord Cavendish and his undersecretary, Burke. English papers claimed the murderers planned and financed their crime in America and placed the ultimate responsibility at the feet of American authorities who had failed to suppress the wild urgings of America's radical Irishmen. Thus, even though agrarian agitation in Ireland gradually disappeared during the summer of 1882, and Lowell worked with some success to close the "Suspects" case, succeeding in having the British release prisoners on condition that they leave Ireland, radical Irish-Americans filled the void and continued to disturb Anglo-American relations.

CHAPTER 7

At the Apex of Power

I   *The Democratic Return to Power*

THE activities of the Irish in America in the early 1880's, created and intensified by the events in Ireland, had obviously pushed Irish interests into the limelight of America's politics. Much of the congressional attention given the "Suspects" case rested firmly upon the knowledge that 1882 was an election year in which each representative and one third of the senators would have to report to the people. White House interest in this Irish issue was also due to the realization that the Irish had clearly emerged as the ruling element in the balance of political power in all-important New York State. Consequently, as the election campaign developed steam toward the end of the summer, both parties fought for the attention of the Irish voter.

In August, 1882, Frelinghuysen pressed the British for the release of all "Suspects" still in British jails. Congressmen made similar demands, while visiting Englishmen constantly commented on the interest both parties showed toward the Irish vote. At the same time, American journalists produced articles dealing with the growing power of the Irish in America to influence American elections and upon the Irish-American tendency to vote for or against a candidate on the basis of his response to the Anglo-Irish struggle.

As the congressional campaign of 1882 progressed, the Republicans gained the allegiance of many Irish leaders, while Democratic platforms in New York, Indiana, and Illinois condemned the Republican administration for permitting American citizens to remain in British jails. Senator John Sherman believed it was easy to convince intelligent Irish voters in Ohio to break with the Democratic party on the question of free trade. This emphasis on Irish troubles continued until election day as claims and counterclaims filled the campaign oratory.

In spite of the Republican efforts, however, the Democrats won control of the House of Representatives. The shift of control did not change the attitude of the new British minister in Washington toward the future. Shortly after the election, he informed the Foreign Office that the Democrats "will pander the Irish vote as did the Republicans."[2]

The actual power of the Irish voter in this campaign is difficult to judge; but professional politicians thought it was considerable, mainly because they believed the events in Ireland had forced the Irish in America into a solid bloc of voters. It was assumed that the Irish would vote for those who sponsored the Irish cause. In the months between the election of 1882 and the presidential campaign of 1884 the politicians continued to believe that such a policy would work to their advantage, particularly because Ireland's troubles continued to receive more than adequate coverage in America's press. For that reason, events in Ireland continued to determine the question of how much political power the Irish in America could muster.

The Ireland of 1883 and 1884 differed sharply from the preceding three years. Parnell had reduced the agitation over land and agrarian difficulties and for two years had isolated himself and his parliamentary party from the politics of violence. The Land League gave way to the low-profile National League; but as Ireland cooled, the radicals both there and in America emerged to dominate the news. With Parnell quiet, the radicals had no effective opposition.

In this situation, the extremists filled the American press with their exploits. British authorities, for instance, made a number of arrests in the Phoenix Park murder case on January 13, 1883. In the trial that followed the informer, James Carey, pictured the "Invincibles" as a secret group of hard-core fanatics dedicated to the assassination of high government officials. He named an Irishman, P. J. Sheridan, then a resident in the United States, as one of the organizers; and the English press immediately demanded Sheridan's extradition. Many Americans equated the "Invincibles" with the violence of the Molly Maguires and thus had little sympathy for men like Sheridan, but even these Americans would not accept his forced return to England because it would mean the extradition of a political prisoner. Rumor had it that Sheridan had hired Gen. Benjamin Butler, then governor of Massachusetts, as his lawyer in case the British officially asked for his extradition. The British minister in Washington cautioned that little would be gained from such an official request since "the complete subserviency of the State Department to the Irish element in New York and the influence it will exercise in this case upon the decision of the Commissioner renders success extremely doubtful." The British minister read the American situation correctly, for the Republican party simply could not afford to antagonize the Irish vote.

While this case attracted American attention, the Irish-American revolutionary society Clan-na-Gael completed plans for a series of terrorist attacks, and on March 15, 1883 a group of Irish-Americans attempted to destroy the Local Government Board building in London with nitroglycerine. The authorities quickly arrested the group and discovered similar explosives near the London *Times* printing office. The British press carried stories that the Fenians had manufactured enough nitroglycerine to destroy England. Parliament quickly passed a new explosives bill, and the queen signed it into law within twenty-four hours.

The sense of panic that such attacks created in London spread in April when James Carey publicly identified James Tynan, then resident in America, as "Number One," the leader of the "Invincibles." The disclosures at the trial of the dynamiters increased the British conviction that they would not be safe until the United States put an end to the plotting of such crimes in America. In May rumors flew that England would ask for extradition of both Tynan and Sheridan.

Americans quickly denounced the ability of the Irish to use American soil to plot these crimes, but no law existed to bridge the gap between crimes planned in America and executed in England. Furthermore, the Irish possessed enough political leverage to guarantee that Congress would refuse to pass any law that would permit the arrest of persons prior to the commission of any crime.

When the cases involving the "Invincibles" and dynamiters ended in convictions in London in the late spring of 1883, it appeared that this radical agitation had run its course and that Irish attempts to force Anglo-American relations into a serious break would cease. Such hopes, however, evaporated on July 29 when an Irishman, James O'Donnell, murdered James Carey, the informer in the "Invincibles" case, on the British liner the *Melrose Castle* as it steamed along the coast of Africa. O'Donnell immediately claimed American citizenship and asked the American minister in

London to appoint counsel for his defense. John F. Finerty, American-born congressman from Chicago's Irish Second District and editor of the Chicago *Citizen*, immediately organized a committee to defend O'Donnell and asked Secretary Frelinghuysen to intervene in his behalf. A few days later Senator John A. Logan, soon to be a candidate for the vice-presidency, and four Illinois representatives made a similar request. This pressure led to a long exchange between the State Department and the American embassy in London, which proved that O'Donnell was not an American citizen, nor had he ever indicated any great desire to become one.

Yet neither President Arthur nor Frelinghuysen could ignore the mounting pressure, and on November 19 the latter ordered Lowell to accept O'Donnell as an American citizen and to seek permission for American counsel to appear in court in O'Donnell's behalf. The British refused this request, tried O'Donnell, found him guilty, and sentenced him to death. The pressures on Arthur again quickly mounted, and he attempted to save O'Donnell from the death sentence with quiet diplomacy, but the British again frustrated these attempts. On December 11 the president personally intervened and asked for a delay of the execution. Again the British refused, and O'Donnell died on December 17, 1883. In spite of their failure to prevent O'Donnell's death, the Irish had reached the highest decision-makers in the government and had forced them to make decisions contrary to the evidence and their better judgment.

The radicals, moreover, refused to stop their plan of terror. The Clan attempted to destroy London's "underground railroad" on October 30, 1883, at 8:00 P.M. causing damage to trains, one station, and serious injury to a number of persons. Elated with their success, the Clan planned a more extensive effort and on February 26, 1884 attempted to destroy four stations of the London, Chatham, and Dover Railroad. Only one device, however, functioned properly. The authorities discovered the others intact, and an examination of the various components proved that they were made in America. One British editor commented that he knew American politicians would do nothing to antagonize the Irish vote, but he did not believe the Irish had sufficient power to determine the policy of the United States. As if to prove this point, President Arthur called for strict enforcement of existing laws concerning the shipment of dynamite by boat. Yet the radical Irish continued their activities. In open defiance of growing American reaction, Patrick Ford announced plans for another collection to finance more attacks, and on May 30 explosions occurred in Saint James Square, Scotland Yard. On the next day authorities found an unexploded black bag containing dynamite at the base of Lord Nelson's monument. American indignation grew, but nothing happened as the nation prepared for a political campaign in which both parties needed the Irish vote.[2]

The Republican administration's approach to Irish issues in 1883 obviously rested upon a desire not to drive Irish voters toward the Democrats, and by the spring of 1884 the party leadership had incorporated this concept into the election campaign. While many Republican dailies claimed the Irish would vote Republican on the protection issue, representatives from twenty-five states assembled in Chicago in May for the first convention of the Irish Republican National League. When the Republican National Convention met to select their candidates, Irish influence led to the selection of Father Charles O'Reilly, treasurer of the Irish National League of America, to offer the opening invocation—the first Catholic priest to perform that service at a Republican convention. In the battle for the nomination the supporters of James G. Blaine claimed their man would capture New York's Irish and, consequently, the state, for two reasons: Blaine had Irish ancestors, and "the dynamite wing of the Irish will go for him because they know he would resist British arrogance and pretentions and protect American citizenship abroad." When Blaine received the nomination, the British minister in Washington, Sir Lionel Sackville-West, reported that if Blaine had to win New York "by pandering the Irish vote, he would not scruple to do so, nor indeed would any other political leader with whom I am acquainted hesitate to take such a course." True to that prediction, Republicans told the Irish why they should vote for Blaine, and the English press condemned them for making such deliberate appeals to the Irish vote.

Blaine's nomination disturbed a significant body of Republicans, who bolted the party, received the name, "Mugwumps," and worked for the nomination of a liberal, high-minded Democrat. Many old-line Democrats felt that such a candidate would help the party capture the White House because he would attract those Republicans who could not support Blaine. Thus, whatever votes Blaine would receive from the Irish would thereby be offset. Patrick

Collins, however, disagreed. He feared such a candidate would drive away as many voters as he would gain. For this reason Collins fought the convention boom for Grover Cleveland and received help from "Honest John" Kelly's Tammany Hall. This anti-Cleveland Irish effort failed; the Democrats nominated the governor of New York, and the battle for the Irish vote commenced.

Republicans claimed that Blaine's mother was Catholic, his cousin, a mother superior in a Catholic convent, and his record anti-English. He opposed free trade, and he defended Irish-American citizens imprisoned in Ireland in 1881-82. On that record he gained the support of Patrick Ford and his *Irish World* and John Devoy's *Irish Nation*. Congressman John Finerty changed party labels and took his Chicago *Citizen* with him. Alexander Sullivan, an old Republican campaigner, used his position as president of the Irish National League of America to turn its August, 1884, convention into a platform for a number of pro-Blaine speakers. Republican Irish-American clubs formed in various parts of the country, and John Devoy, a leading voice in the Clan-na-Gael, formed an Association for the Protection of American Industry. James Brady, another old Republican-Irish voice from Virginia, took the stump for Blaine, while with some friends Patrick Ford, editor of the New York *Irish World*, organized a great rally for their man in New York. Irish-American Blaine-Logan Associations were formed, and many commentators predicted large numbers of Irishmen moving toward the Republican banner. Never have Republicans worked so hard for Irish voters.

At first the Democrats responded with no great alarm. John Boyle O'Reilly kept his Boston *Pilot* on the Democratic side, while the New York *Irish-American* fought to make its readers aware of Republican lies about Cleveland and the truth about Blaine. Democratic papers claimed Blaine's record as secretary of state proved he would lead the nation to war and many argued that he had never defended the Irish "Suspects." Luckily, the Democrats also discovered that Cleveland had his share of Irish blood. His mother's name was O'Neil. Yet these efforts did not stem the tide. Cleveland decided to come to terms with Patrick Collins and called the Boston congressman to the governor's mansion in Albany. What was said was never disclosed, but after the meeting Collins delivered a masterful speech in which he carefully refuted each of the Republican arguments against Cleveland. Democrats reproduced the speech and delivered it to every Irish community in the country.

The struggle continued; but by October it was clear New York would decide the issue and both candidates concentrated their efforts there. The Republicans needed the Irish to offset the Mugwump defection, while the Democrats did all they could to hold both. The election came, and the returns slowly arrived at the headquarters of the respective candidates. In the end, Cleveland carried New York State and with it the White House by only 1,193 votes.

The Irish believed that they had given Cleveland the White House, and they asked for rewards on that basis, They first wanted Patrick Collins in the cabinet, but Cleveland could not pay so high a price. Once in the White House, however, he did grant the Irish a sizable number of lesser offices. William Roberts, the leader of the Senate faction of the Fenians in 1866, became minister to Chile, while S. S. Cox was appointed minister to Turkey. Michael Phelan, brother of the editor of the Saint Louis *Western Watchman*, received the consulship at Halifax, and Anthony M. Keiley, president of the Irish Catholic Benevolent Union, was appointed minister to Italy. Other members of the Union received important positions as the organization's influence reached the national level for the first time. The Irish had obviously learned how to advance in America—on the strength of political power.[3]

Shortly after the election a split in the Clan-na-Gael developed when John Devoy called for an end to the dynamite campaign; yet Alexander Sullivan ignored this call and made the drastic mistake of going so far that the American public's dislike for England could not offset their dislike of terrorism. In early December two Clan men attempted to destroy the second arch of the London Bridge. They failed and died in the attempt. In January, 1885, simultaneous attempts to damage the Tower of London and the House of Commons led to near hysteria in London. Americans now bitterly condemned such use of dynamite, and many held Blaine responsible because he had catered to the wild Irish during the campaign. State legislatures quickly debated and passed new dynamite bills, while George F. Edmunds introduced a similar measure in the United States Senate. Senator Thomas F. Bayard, soon to become secretary of state, introduced a resolution condemning the twin attacks. It passed 63 to 1. Americans had finally taken a stand against international terrorism. Fearful of the ramifications of the American reaction, numerous moderate Irish politicians condemned the dynamite policy and claimed that only a few Irish-Americans supported such schemes.

This reaction among the American people and the moderate Irish leaders helped those who wished to remove Sullivan from the leadership of the Clan. It also meant the end of the dynamite campaign. Even Patrick Ford changed the name of his new special fund for revolutionary activity to make it appear less violent. In short, by the summer of 1885 the Irish in America were as quiet as their relatives on the other side of the Atlantic.[4]

II *Cleveland's First Administration*

The relative calm in Anglo-Irish relations in 1885 stemmed directly from the electoral reforms of late 1884 that gave agricultural workers the right to vote. This meant that in the next Parliament Parnell and his Home Rule party would control at least 85 seats and possibly the balance of power between the major parties. Thus, both the English and the Irish patiently awaited the general elections scheduled for December, 1885. The suspense mounted during the fall campaign and did not end until the returns gave the Liberals 335 seats, the Conservatives 249, and the Home Rulers 86. Neither party could rule without Parnell. He stood at the pinnacle of his power, and the Irish in America experienced a new surge of hope for the fulfillment of their dream.

Parliament met on January 21, 1886, with Home Rule in the air, and in mid-March Gladstone introduced his Home Rule Bill for Ireland. Parliament debated the issue for three months, and when the bill failed Gladstone took the issue to the people by dissolving Parliament and calling for new elections. In a fierce campaign he and Parnell lost. The Liberal-Unionist and Conservative alliance returned to London with a majority of 118 seats. Home Rule had had a short, quick life of six months.[5]

Though it came and went rapidly, Home Rule, while it existed, excited the Irish in America as few issues had. Radicals and moderates, Republicans and Democrats all united behind Parnell who kept Patrick Egan, the old treasurer of the Land League and now the president of the Irish National League of America, well informed of his plans, and the masses again responded with money. When the events in January, 1886, led to the Home Rule Bill, many saw the hope of years approaching reality, and the events of the spring only increased these hopes.

That intensity of hope explains the utter bewilderment that followed the failure of June and July. Fortunately, Egan had arranged for a meeting of the Irish National League in Chicago in the middle of August, and the call for unity filled Irish circles. The meeting was crucial, for without Irish-American support Parnell had no power, and without Parnell, Gladstone was helpless. The convention opened with a struggle between those who, like Sullivan, wished to return to guerrilla warfare and those who wished to follow Parnell's parliamentary leadership. Parnell's emissaries, William O'Brien and Michael Davitt, convinced Egan and Ford that a dynamite campaign of the old order was unnecessary and dangerous. The convention then endorsed a moderate platform in support of Parnell's leadership; Egan resigned, and the delegates elected John Fitzgerald of Lincoln, Nebraska, to succeed to the presidency. Father O'Reilly continued as treasurer, and the money again flowed to Ireland.[6]

This particular convention came at another crucial point in American politics. As the people prepared for off-year congressional elections, Blaine entered the campaign with a denunciation of the Cleveland administration, particularly the secretary of state, for being pro-British. In June, 1886, he delivered a strong speech in support of Irish Home Rule and in the fall returned to Irish grievances. This activity brought to the fore the whole question of the 1884 election and Blaine's appeal in that campaign to the radical Irish. The partisan press debated that effort, and a few papers accused Blaine of supporting dynamite criminals. One daily claimed he wanted to fight a "jingo campaign [in 1886] . . . like the one that had captured a number of hot-headed Irishmen, but that it alienated some business interests which did not want the tail of the British Lion twisted." Blaine ignored these attacks and continued his appeals to the Irish. At one point, the Saint Louis *Post Dispatch* argued he would angle for the Apache Indian vote by discovering "a streak of Indian blood in his veins, as soon as they would register as citizens of Florida."[7]

While the election campaign clearly indicated that the Irish vote remained a major issue in Blaine's strategy, another issue smoldered below the surface of public debate. For some time prior to 1886 Anglo-American diplomats had shown concern over the question of extradition of criminals, and, when Bayard entered office in 1885, he ordered the new minister in London to reopen negotiations on the matter.

These led to a new treaty, signed on June 25, 1885. Americans received the right to seek extradition of those who defaulted on debts and embezzled funds and fled to the safety of Canada. The British received the right to demand custody of those who caused malicious injury to property and persons with explosives. At first this British right did not seem too strange since a similar clause appeared in an extradition treaty signed with Japan in that same month which quickly received Senate approval with little debate. Other treaties negotiated in the next few years also contained similar clauses, and none of these generated any immediate violent reaction in the American population. The English treaty, however, aroused the wrath of the Irish because they saw it as a clear attempt to send dynamite Irishmen back to British jails.

The battle erupted in July, and the Irish, in spite of the support for the treaty in the American banking community, forced the Senate to postpone ratification. For the next two years at the start of each session all elements of the Irish-American community, including such solid Democratic and moderate Irishmen as John Boyle O'Reilly, opposed confirmation of this treaty.[8]

In the middle 1880's the ability of the Irish to influence the Senate rested upon their political control of certain American cities and that unique political balance at the national level that existed during the decade. As long as the Irish ruled certain cities and both parties needed their votes, their influence would be dominant. The English saw this clearly and often clutched at any ray of hope that the Irish would lose their power in America. At one point, the London *Times* argued that Irish power in America was waning because in 1880 they constituted a lower percentage of the foreign-born population than in 1870. One American reader of that article, however, argued the opposite, and claimed that American politicians

pander to the ruling Celtic class among us and I can perceive no emancipation from such rule in the near future. Just enough Irish act with the Republican party or constantly promise to do so, to prevent the Republican leaders and press from saying anything disagreeable about them. A considerable number of Irish in New York, Chicago, Albany, and

Buffalo, and a few other cities voted for Blaine (while voting the rest of the Democratic ticket) and talk about doing it again in 1888 in still greater numbers, and this hope makes the Republican leaders smile on Home Rulers and causes Democratic politicians to hug the Celtic nationalists all the closer to their bosoms lest they may lose them in the next presidential struggle.[9]

This power at the national level, of course, ultimately rested upon the cohesiveness of the Irish, and that in turn rested upon what happened in Ireland. In the months that followed the first attempt at Home Rule, the economy of Ireland again failed, and Irish leaders made frequent appeals to the Irish in America for money to prevent evictions, while Parnell and his Liberal allies used what parliamentary power they possessed to stop evictions and prevent coercive legislation. They made some headway against evictions, but they failed to prevent efforts by the Conservatives to suppress Ireland. In the summer of 1887 Arthur Balfour, chief secretary for Ireland, suppressed the National League with new legislation and jailed many of the leaders. Parnell refused to take the path toward violence and decided to maintain the middle road, without which he would have no link with Gladstone and the Liberals. Thus, Ireland again had her problems, but this time her leaders urged caution and moderation.[10]

III   *The Election of 1888*

Parnell's policy kept Ireland cool in 1887 and 1888, eliminated any possibility that radicals would again control events and thus permitted the Irish in America to concentrate upon the presidential election. The election year started with a debate on the extradition treaty, and again the Senate refused to ratify it. At the same time, the United States and England signed a treaty that ended the growing animosity arising from the northeast fisheries. This second treaty quickly became a political football as the Republicans claimed it proved the pro-British attitude of the Democratic administration. The Republican appeal to both Irish and native American animosities received added impetus when Cleveland announced he would fight the campaign on the tariff question. Republicans could now appeal to the Irish on an issue Blaine had used as early as October, 1880. Again Cleveland had to cultivate the Boston congressman, Patrick Collins, and his friends with special care.

Thus, when Collins went to Cleveland to oppose the nomination of the then minister to England, Edward Phelps, to the Supreme Court, Cleveland listened. When the party met in convention in Saint Louis in 1888 to nominate Cleveland for a second term in the White House, Collins served as permanent chairman. In that capacity he delivered an address on the principles of the Democratic party which the party reproduced and used extensively in Irish wards. The convention, of course, endorsed Cleveland and accepted a platform which called for a reduction of the tariff and, among other things, Home Rule for Ireland.

Meanwhile, Blaine had virtually withdrawn from the Republican race in spite of Patrick Ford's urging that he run again. When the Republicans met on June 19, 1888, no one could predict the outcome. In the end, Benjamin Harrison of Indiana gained the presidential nomination, and Levi P. Morton of New York was nominated for the vice-presidency. Republicans gleefully accepted the tariff as the issue and also found room in their platform for Home Rule for Ireland.

For the next four months the two parties fought to attract Irish voters. The Republicans used their radical Irish allies while the Democrats dealt with the more moderate elements in Irish-American circles. Both sides used Anglo-American difficulties, and both accused each other of being responsible for the dynamite clause in the 1886 extradition treaty with England. The campaign again settled in New York. The famous disclosure on the eve of the election that the British minister in Washington, Sir Sackville-West, wanted the Democrats to win, led to his swift dismissal and expulsion from the country. What effect this tragic and comic incident had upon the election, of course, is difficult to determine, but Harrison did win New York by 14,000 votes—and the White House—although Cleveland had the majority of the nation's voters on his side.[11]

Again the Irish claimed their votes had decided the issue, and President Harrison had to find places for Republican Irishmen. Patrick Egan, the old Land League treasurer in 1882, who had arrived in America in 1883, received the post of minister to Chile where he replaced the old Fenian, William Roberts. Numerous minor posts went to loyal Irishmen, and on May 22 Blaine, now secretary of state, arranged a meeting between Harrison and Patrick Ford with the remark that "it will do much good in certain important directions." As late as 1891 Blaine appointed an Irishman as secretary of the legation in Bogotá because the Catholic priest in Brooklyn who suggested his name controlled many votes, and this "might be worthwhile in the next election."[12]

By then, however, the whole context of Irish influence in American politics had changed. The agitation in Ireland suffered a devastating blow when Parnell fell from power and died prematurely in 1891. Ireland had lost the voice that had dominated her affairs for a decade and generated the events that kept the cohesiveness of the Irish in America alive.[13]

At the same time, Irish nationalism in America suffered a serious blow. A division in the Clan-na-Gael had begun in late 1884, and by 1888 the Sullivan wing felt compelled to adjust their differences with the group led by Dr. Patrick H. Cronin. On May 4, 1889, four Sullivan supporters murdered Cronin in Chicago. The resulting arrests and public trial shocked Americans and Irish-Americans alike. The radical faction had once again overstepped the bounds of American hospitality, and the Clan collapsed. By 1890 it had little influence in Irish-American circles.[14]

Finally, the change in administrations caused a shift in the American political scene. Upon entering office, the Republicans took steps to reduce Anglo-American tensions, and the Anglophobia that had existed during the 1880's and had done so much to increase Irish power diminished noticeably. The British also indicated a desire to reduce Anglo-American tensions in the aftermath of the Sackville-West incident, with the appointment of a senior diplomat, Julian Pauncefote, as their minister in Washington.

These events in Ireland, England, and America greatly reduced the ability of Irish-Americans to influence politics at the national level, though a degree of power was retained. In February, 1889, for instance, the Senate finally rejected the extradition treaty with England, and in the months that followed Blaine negotiated a new treaty that did not contain the objectionable clause. Then in the elections of 1892 the Democrats again leaned heavily upon the Irish. William F. Harrity, an early graduate of La Salle College and a Democratic force in Philadelphia, became the party's national chairman, and when Cleveland won he gave Patrick Collins what he wanted, the consul-generalship at London. It was a strange twist of fate that an old Fenian warrior of the 1866 battles should return to

England with diplomatic immunity.[15] Yet the election of 1892 did not have the significance for Irish-Americans that the campaigns of 1884 and 1888 had had. Ireland was simply too quiet, and the Irish in America lacked that unanimity of interest that had characterized the 1880's.[16] An era of power at the national political level had ended for this pressure group. The Irish in America would not regain that old sense of power for twenty years.

CHAPTER 8

Twenty Years of Transition

I *Local Politics*

IN the twenty years that followed the election of 1892 conditions both in Ireland and America failed to give the Irish in America an opportunity to intervene in the Anglo-Irish struggle or to use that struggle to increase their power in American society. The fall and premature death of Parnell left Ireland in a state of political bankruptcy by dividing the Home Rule party into two bitterly hostile factions. Land warfare and agrarian agitation declined rapidly as relative peace returned to the countryside.[1]

Meanwhile, in America the election of 1896 decisively ended that "era of no decision" which had given the Irish so much political power and marked the Republican emergence as the dominant party in the country. The return of prosperity shortly after William McKinley entered office confirmed that trend, and in 1900 the party managers showed little fear of the Democratic opposition. A campaign for the "Full Dinner Pail" gave the Republicans another victory and four more years in power. McKinley's assassination placed Theodore Roosevelt in the White House, and his capture of the Progressive movement meant another four years of Republican administration. In 1908 William Taft had little difficulty in making it four Republican elections in succession, and not until 1910 did the nation again experience growing division on issues that would provide political opportunities for well-organized minorities. In the fourteen years from 1896 to 1910 Republican bosses did not find the Irish votes necessary for success at the polls.[2]

At the same time, America's diplomats discovered little use for Irish-Americans in their dealings with the outside world. The widening of American interests that followed the Spanish-American War ended an age in which relations with England dominated America's foreign policy and, thus, the nuisance value of Irish-American agitation against England was lessened. Too, conditions on both sides of the Atlantic led to a rapprochement between the two countries which began at the close of the Venezuelan crisis of 1895, continued through negotiations for American control of a Panama Canal, and closed with a series of negotiations in the Taft Administration that ended long-standing problems such as the fate of the fur seals in the Bering Sea and American fishing rights in Canadian waters. Finally, America's power relationship with the outside world underwent a fundamental change at the turn of the century. In the 1880's, when America possessed limited power and her politicians permitted internal political considerations to determine policy, her diplomats could speak with relative abandon. However, by 1898 America had grown enormously both in military and industrial strength, and American diplomats could no longer speak recklessly. They had to measure their public statements carefully, for the world took their words seriously. In that new situation minority groups in general had little real influence upon policy.[3]

If the American Irish lost their ability to influence national politics as decisively as they had in the 1880's, they did not suffer any great setback on the local level. Although the Irish percentage of the foreign-born in America continued to drop in the years after 1890, the established Irish-Americans quickly learned how to take advantage of the later waves of immigrants. Their entrenchment in city government gave them control of both jobs and money which they freely used to insure they would remain in power. They could speak the language which many of the new immigrants could not, and their high degree of organization meant that only a similarly organized group could drive them from their seats of power. In addition, the heavy concentration of the Irish in the cities of the Northeast meant that the national leadership of the Democratic party would at least have to continue to cater to the Irish bosses in those towns. Thus in the 1890's Irish power at the local level grew as cities like Philadelphia, Brooklyn, Jersey City, Buffalo, Chicago, Milwaukee, Saint Louis, and San Francisco fell under their sway.[4]

During these years the Irish took possession of Boston. Patrick Collins had led the first assault on the domination of the city by the old Puritan classes in the late 1870's and early 1880's. His service in Congress and in the Cleveland presidential campaigns added immeasurably to his stature at the national level. It was to be expected that Cleveland would give him the post of his choice in

1893, but McKinley's election four years later meant that Collins had to return to the United States. His career on the national level had ended.

When he returned to Boston he discovered that Irish power had grown in his absence. That power gave him an opportunity to continue his political career. For a number of reasons he decided to run for the mayor's office in 1902, and he won handily. His reelection to a second term cemented Irish control of the city. When he left city hall all political offices in Boston were held by Irishmen. The transformation from the English Puritans to the Irish Catholics was complete as such colorful figures as "Honey Fitz," the grandfather of John F. Kennedy, and James M. Curley followed Collins in the mayor's office. Even Henry Cabot Lodge, heir to the older political tradition, quickly learned to forget his anti-immigrant feeling as he sought the political power of the Irish in his many campaigns for the United States Senate. On the basis of the work done by Collins and his generation, America's Irish ruled Boston until well into the 1960's. [5]

Alongside of the Irish capture of Boston, their continued domination of Tammany meant that New York would remain the focal point for Irish politicians and the example to be followed by all. "Honest John" Kelly's death in 1885 suddenly left Tammany without a strong leader, and the majority of district leaders favored a system of rule by committee. Yet on the day after Kelly's funeral Richard Croker simply walked into "Honest John's" office and took his desk. He ruled the "Wigwam" for sixteen years.

Croker, born in County Cork, Ireland, sailed to America with his parents in the first frightful year of the famine, 1846. His father found shelter in Central Park's shantytown and soon got a job from Tammany Hall. Croker grew up in the tenement-ridden East Side and learned to survive in the ever-present world of gang warfare. In command of the Tunnel Gang he developed a reputation in the 1860's for supplying "honest" repeaters. He himself voted for one candidate seventeen times in one day. His work for the party gained the attention of Sheriff Jimmy O'Brien, and in the struggles that followed the fall of the Tweed Ring he sided with "Honest John" Kelly. Although he had serious problems in the late 1870's, including a trial for murder in which he won acquittal, he maintained his relationship with Kelly and became his right-hand man. From that position Croker succeeded to command of the Wigwam.

The new boss of New York had no interest in living the relatively quiet life of his predecessor. Croker wanted to live a flamboyant life, and Tammany would give him the necessary money. He quickly consolidated his power over the Wigwam itself and destroyed the remaining power of the Swallowtails by winning the mayoralty election of 1886 and by supporting Grover Cleveland in the 1888 campaign. In control of Tammany and without opposition in the city, he ran a trusted lieutenant for the mayor's office and won. By 1890 Croker owned the city.

The style of the new boss differed considerably from that of earlier ones, but Croker continued to use the organization techniques developed during the 1880's and also created an extraordinary social service system. To insure continued power, his Tammany "braves" earnestly cultivated the new immigrants. The boss carefully selected the district captains to insure that they could serve the needs of their districts. They had to know their people, and by the end of the decade one would find a captain in the front pew of a Catholic church on one day and in the front pew of a synagogue the next. He worked twenty hours a day seven days a week and never asked for anything in exchange for numerous favors, except on election day.

Croker, of course, used patronage freely to help keep his machine well oiled, and he did not outlaw the less respectable means of collecting money. New York in the Gay Nineties was an open city where prostitution ran rampant under the protection of the Tammany-controlled police department. Gambling and other illegal activities flourished, and although numerous efforts to correct the situation made some headway they failed to create any permanent change. In 1892 the public first learned of the widespread crime that could not have flourished without protection. In March, 1894, as a result of a division between Croker and the Republican Tom Platt, the state legislature appointed the Lexow Committee to investigate police corruption in New York. The result of the year-long investigation shocked New Yorkers as nothing had since the Tweed Ring. Croker and Tammany lost the 1894 election, and the boss sailed to England for a three-year exile, leaving an aide to control things in his absence.

Croker never personally engaged in these questionable activities or gained any profit from them. He always claimed that he had earned his fortune from "honest graft." Businessmen who had to deal with the city often gave him useful information about the stock market. His real estate firm proved quite profitable, and in the early 1890's he had homes and stud farms in New York, Florida, and England. Thus, when he went into exile he had the means to live well.

Croker returned to New York on September 7, 1897. Quickly regaining control of Tammany, he ran his man for mayor and won. With firm control of the city, he decided to make a bid for control of the Democratic party in the state. In the 1898 campaign for governor, however, Croker's candidate lost to the Republican Teddy Roosevelt. Two years later, a second McKinley victory destroyed any hope that Croker had of controlling the state. Then in 1901 a new investigation showed that "dirty" graft had again returned to the city. Reformers defeated the Tammany slate, and Croker again sailed from New York. He lived the remainder of his life in Ireland. When he died in 1922, the soldiers of the IRA escorted his body to its final resting place. An Irish lad had come home to rest.

While Croker lived in retirement, the reigns of power in Tammany fell into the hands of another Irish-Catholic who was to benefit from the Golden Years of Tammany rule. Born of Irish immigrants, Charles Murphy grew up in the rough-and-tumble of the Gas House district, where he eventually leased his first saloon. By the early 1890's he had four more saloons, had entered politics—and he attended church every Sunday.

This seemingly dull man gained power and, by shrewd balancing of the forces that now made the city and by carefully cultivating the finest stable of candidates in American political history, Murphy ruled the Wigwam and the city until his death in 1924. In those twenty-three years, the city filled the old communities with all kinds of new immigrants, and Murphy's machine cared for them. He brought to the fore of American politics such names as Al Smith, Robert F. Wagner, Edward J. Flynn, and the incredible Jimmy Walker. In all those years he carefully managed his own affairs and lived the quiet life of an "Honest John" Kelly. Numerous enemies, both in and out of Tammany, attempted to remove him from power.

They included such men as Franklin D. Roosevelt and Woodrow Wilson, but none succeeded.

After years of carefully creating his winning margins in the city and the state, Murphy set out to establish a new record—to put Al Smith in the White House. He carefully groomed his man, but on the eve of the 1924 Democratic Convention, Murphy died. His funeral rivaled that of General Grant. Fifty thousand people lined New York's streets, and six thousand pushed into Saint Patrick's Cathedral. A man and an era had ended. It would not return.[6]

II *Church*

The history of Tammany Hall from the Civil War to the 1920's is obviously a history of an institution that enabled poor Irish immigrants to find a way out of the ghetto into the middle- and upper-class dream world that was America. In those same years the Irish used another vehicle for the trip up and out—the Catholic church.

The relationship between the Irish immigrant and the Catholic church began long before he stepped onto American soil. From the time of Patrick, the Irish and the church had existed as an inseparable unity, and British attempts to impose a Protestant religion on Ireland strengthened that relationship. The bitter economic and political struggle that was the lot of the Irish in the eighteenth and nineteenth centuries had a religious counterpart that added to the bitterness. To be Irish was to be Catholic.

That characteristic followed the immigrant to America. Prior to the famine immigration, Catholics constituted a distinct minority ruled by an Anglo-American clergy but without an effective voice in an ocean of Protestantism. At the same time, relatively few Americans paid any attention to the Roman church except to keep Catholics out of American society. Catholics did play a minor role in the American Revolution and the political battles that followed the writing of the Constitution, but not until the early Jackson years did Americans give them any real attention. Too small and too inconspicuous to constitute a threat to the American Protestant majority, the Catholics in America concentrated on building concrete expressions of their existence in America—their churches.

This situation changed slowly in the 1830's both for Americans and for the church. The Irish migrations that followed the

Napoleonic Wars gradually increased the number of Catholics in America. Consequently, the feeling that these newcomers could threaten Protestant America grew. In the 1830's outbursts of anti-Catholic feeling occurred, and these increased rapidly in number and intensity in the early 1840's as more Irishmen arrived. The riots in Philadelphia in 1844 led to pitched battles between the Catholic Irish and the Protestant Americans. Then the migrations of the famine fueled the anti-Catholic movement into the Know-Nothing party. The struggle that followed in the 1850's produced the modern Catholic church in America, an Irish church which lasted for a century.

In these anti-Catholic battles the Irish supplied the masses. In 1840, for instance, only 663,000 Americans claimed adherence to Catholicism. By 1850 that figure had increased by 1 million and in the decade that preceded the Civil War another 600,000 were added. In 1860 the Catholic church claimed a membership of 2.2 million of which 1.6 million were Irish. No wonder the Know-Nothings wanted to stop the Irish, but by 1860 they had lost that battle.

While the Irish filled the ranks of the church, they also captured the leadership roles. By the time of the Civil War all the prominent voices that spoke for Catholicism carried Irish names. Not until the 1890's did the domination of the hierarchy face a serious challenge. In 1886 thirty-five of the ninety-six American bishops were Irish. The Germans, who ranked second, could count only fifteen. In addition, those thirty-five American bishops held the more powerful sees and spoke with the most powerful authority. No wonder the average American came to see Irish and Catholic as synonymous and to use them as one word.[7]

Meanwhile, the church itself began to feel and act upon the political power of the famine immigrants. The incomparable career of John Hughes, archbishop of New York, reflected the change in attitudes of Catholics in America. In the 1840's and 1850's he led his Irish flock against nativist attacks, while in the 1860's politicians from Washington as well as New York sought his advice and assistance.

The struggle for parochial education, in which Hughes played a significant role, clearly reflected the changing nature of the church's place in America. As early as 1829 the bishops asked their people to build parish schools to preserve the faith, and the Irish immediately answered by building them. In 1835 Irishmen forced the town of Lowell, Massachusetts, to incorporate two Irish schools (buildings and teachers supplied by the Irish) into its school system. Numerous other compatible arrangements developed in other locales, but the nativist controversy of the 1840's soon killed these. In New York and Philadelphia the bishops answered with a demand for public funds and the end of the forced reading of the King James version of the Bible in public schools. Both sides fought pitched battles over these issues.

Nativist activity gradually declined toward the end of the 1850's, and during the Civil War the bishops, using the political power of the church, forced local school authorities into various plans that granted public assistance to Catholic schools. The greatest success in this area came in the 1870's, and many of these agreements lasted until the revival of nativism in the 1890's with the appearance of the American Protective Association. The power of the church to demand and receive such assistance, of course, clearly rested upon the political power of the Irish vote. The Irish-Catholic church had learned its lesson well in the crises of the Know-Nothing party. Safety in America demanded large numbers of bloc voters.

The church influenced the lives of the Irish immigrants in many ways. The family unit was really the center of their religious life. There they said their prayers before and after meals, in the morning when they awoke, and in the evening as they went to bed. At least once a week they knelt with the family to recite the rosary. The Irish mother, who wanted her sons and daughters to enter religious life, saw to it that the children went to a parochial school. Where this was not possible, they trained their children in the laws of the church and prepared them for the sacraments. In that atmosphere the young grew up under the spell of enormous awe of the local priest. He had the keys to heaven. That sense of authority carried into the homes where the father was literally king.

The authoritarian and God-centered atmosphere of the Irish family continued long into the twentieth century, and much of its strength rested upon the attitude of Americans. Native Americans felt superior to these immigrants, not only because the Irish could work only at the lowest of jobs, but more because of their blind obedience to their priests. The Americans felt that the inferior parochial school education and the obviously second-class status of Irish-Catholic-supported higher education only continued that kind of narrow-minded thinking. The Irish, themselves, often agreed. How could Boston College compete with Harvard University? In this sense their experience in America remained little different from their experience in Ireland.

Yet the church continued to grow, but not without problems. The continued domination by the Irish caused a number of internal dissensions, mainly with the growing number of German Catholics. By the 1880's this erupted into an open battle among the bishops when the Germans wanted their own "national" church instead of the regular, or "Irish," church. The demands for foreign-language churches grew in the 1890's as the new immigrants from Eastern and Southern Europe arrived.

This particular problem became part of the larger issue of Americanism. Some of the Irish prelates fought the trend of autonomy for foreign-language churches. They wanted an American church that Americans would accept. In the broad struggle over Americanization, Irish prelates divided; some of the more conservative bishops felt that some positions of Americanism bordered on heresy. The Pope sided with them and ended the infighting when he issued *Testem Benevolentiae*. That decision, by supporting the orthodox position and avoiding change, may very possibly have helped to continue the Irish domination of the church.[7]

In the same decade the Irish and their church faced new opposition from the old American impulse, nativism. Founded in the Midwest in 1887, the American Protective Association rapidly spread to other parts of the country and eventually involved hundreds of thousands of Americans. APA activities led to a serious and violent clash with Boston's Irish during one Fourth of July parade. Fortunately, the association quickly died after the election of 1896 and the return of prosperity which followed.[8] Irish fears of renewed persecutions also disappeared as the average Irishman found himself slowly assimilated into American life after 1890. That decreased the need to find safety in numbers as his ancestors did in the 1850's.

III *Struggle for Respectability*

During these years of change the Irish also found themselves in competition with other immigrant groups. When the Italians began to arrive in the 1890's, they gained the animosity of America's "shanty" Irish who saw the newcomers as competitors for their jobs and for their homes as well. Italians in turn found that the Irish ruled, not only their churches, but their city. The inevitable battles between the two groups followed. Irish churchmen and politicians condemned these clashes, but the bitterness did not decrease until the Irish moved out of the old neighborhood and up the economic ladder, a process both long and difficult.

A similar bitterness characterized Irish relations with Polish-Americans in many cities, while in Brooklyn, New York, and Boston the Irish looked upon Jews as the enemy. Anti-Semitism added fuel to the battles in these cities, but the fundamental animosity between the groups rested upon social and economic conditions. The same factors obviously prompted the Irish to participate in the battles against Chinese and Japanese immigration on the West Coast, but the successful flight of some Irish out of their ghettos also intensified these struggles.[9]

By the 1890's the distinction between the "lace-curtain" and "shanty" Irish was clear, and those who had not yet made the climb did not wish any competition. The mentality of the famine Irish had changed, although as a group they still bitterly hated the English. Yet they found much less prejudice and oppression than had greeted their parents in the 1850's. America no longer despised them, but rather gave them the chance to achieve the better life they sought. They were, in effect, becoming respectable, not as individuals and exceptions to the rule, but as a group and as the rule.

Their growing respectability had profound effect upon their organizations. Part of the decline of the Irish Catholic Benevolent Union resulted from a change in Irish tastes during the 1890's. The concept of benevolence lost its appeal since the economic position of the Irish as a group had improved considerably, and they wanted a different kind of national organization. Thus, they moved toward the Ancient Order of Hibernians and its clubs, where they could buy their favorite beverages at bargain prices and enjoy each other's company. At the same time, the Hibernians found a substitute for benevolence in a new form of militancy which attempted to remove from America's image of her Irish citizens all shades of misconduct. For twenty-five years that effort made the Hibernians a powerful voice in Irish America.[10]

The rising sense of respectability also prompted the formation of the American Irish Historical Society in Boston in 1897. With headquarters in New York under the leadership of Michael J. O'Brien, the society soon published a journal and filled its pages with stories about the Irish contribution to American history. Many questioned much of what was written, especially O'Brien's claims of Irish participation in the American Revolution, but those stories did reflect the Irish desire to proclaim themselves an integral part of American society and establish their right to respectability.[11]

This changing concept of themselves emerges quite clearly in their reaction to the stage. Prior to the 1890's, the Irish had produced a large number of stage types which played before audiences from one end of the country to the other. The famous works of Harrigan and Hart constantly portrayed the story of poor Irish on the way up. Significantly, however, Harrigan's last success came in 1890, and that stage type declined rapidly in the 1890's. Some still attempted that old theme, but the Irish in America in the 1890's quickly came to the realization that they had to correct the impressions created by these stage stereotypes, especially the image of an Irishman as a drunk. In a concrete fashion and as an expression of the militancy that meant so much to them, the Hibernians formed a special committee to remove the stage Irishman in all of his ignorance and stupidity from the American scene. On the eve of World War I, their determination to create a new ideal led to a wild hostility to the productions that grew out of the Irish Literary Renaissance—the works of Yeats, Synge, and the whole Abbey Theatre Movement. They saved their greatest blows for Synge's *Playboy of the Western World* which they claimed clearly distorted their ancestors.[12]

If the Irish lost their interest in the old stage, they did not lose their love of song and poetry. Songs continued to tell their story, but they kept many to themselves. A few, like "Sweet Rosie O'Grady" and "My Wild Irish Rose," became genuinely American. Other Irishmen wrote purely American songs. Patrick Gilmore wrote the popular song of World War I, "When Johnny Comes Marching Home," and Victor Herbert captured the imagination of a generation. Their poetry appeared as early as the 1850's, but it circulated only among the Irish until in the 1880's and 1890's the poems of Reverend John Ryan captured the heart of America. His "Conquered Banner" and "The Sword of Robert E. Lee" are still found in schoolbooks. John Boyle O'Reilly, editor of the Boston

Pilot, won serious acclaim for his poems, which ranged far beyond Irish topics. [13]

Acclaim as songwriters and poets, however, did not make for a great reputation in the world of serious works. A few Irish-Americans did publish more serious works, but Maurice Francis Egan, another early graduate of La Salle College and a prolific writer, complained bitterly that most of the books published by Catholics were of extremely poor quality. Egan felt that those who came before the famine had higher tastes and that the post-famine Irish wanted only books on Irish history or on the church. Yet, Egan's own career would indicate that his indictment was not accurate, that an Irishman of literary talent could capture a place in New York literary circles. After a later and successful career as a newspaperman for Catholic papers, he went to Notre Dame to teach English and then moved to Catholic University in Washington. There he became a close friend of Theodore Roosevelt and gained an appointment as ambassador to Denmark. His more than forty volumes include his reflections on European diplomacy on the eve of World War I. [14]

If Egan's success in literary circles marked a change, American fiction confirmed it. Whereas prior to the 1890's only Irish-American writers employed Irish themes, American novelists began to use them with greater frequency in the years that followed. Upton Sinclair used Irish characters in many of his works as did Theodore Dreiser and Stephen Crane, but the real Irish invasion of American fiction did not come until after World War I.

The Irish penetration of the world of sports by the 1890's served as another sign of their growing respectability. Their spirit of competition and their love of fighting had always driven them into athletics. In the early and middle years of the century they played games imported from the old country. In time, they accepted America's games, and by the 1880's and early 1890's, Irish names dominated boxing. John L. Sullivan defeated Paddy Ryan for the heavyweight championship of the world in 1882. Ten years later he lost his title to "Gentleman Jim" Corbett, who ruled during the 1890's, only to lose the title to Jim Jeffries in 1900. The extent of Irish control of boxing caused others to fight under Irish names simply to gain recognition. Not until the 1930's could Italians in South Boston fight under their own names. [15]

Irishmen dominated other sports, including the national pastime, baseball. Michael J. Kelly, who died in 1894, inspired the popular song, "Slide, Kelly, Slide," while in the twentieth century John McGraw and Charles A. Comiskey built baseball empires in New York and Chicago, respectively. Mickey Cochrane, the game's greatest catcher, inspired many young men; while the success of such players as Hugh Duffy, who batted .438 in 1894; John Joseph Doyle, an infielder in the 1890's; Peter J. Daniels, a great pitcher; and Roger Patrick Bresnahan, the "Duke of Tralee" and battery mate of the great Christy Mathewson, contributed to the rising image of Irish respectability. The Irish played American football and gave Notre Dame, a school founded by a French priest, the name the "Fighting Irish." Various Irish-American athletic clubs sponsored track-and-field events. In 1895 Thomas Burke won the quarter-mile race in an international event in New York between American and English athletes. Later he won two Olympic championships. Michael Charles Murphy, from Massachusetts, became a famous coach at Yale and Pennsylvania and on two occasions coached America's Olympic teams.

The Irish produced heroes of the sports world, and they also produced those who could describe their feats. John Kiernan in New York and Thomas Dorgan in San Francisco wrote on all sports topics, while James Dawson was the boxing editor of the New York *Times*, where he worked for forty-four years. Peter Finley Dunne, the creator of the colorful Mr. Dooley, also appeared on the sports page. [16]

At the same time, more and more Irish-Americans were reaching positions of respectability in other fields. John B. McDonald of New York built miles of railroads and a New York subway. When he died in New York in 1913, the subways stopped for two minutes during the funeral Mass sung at Saint Patrick's. John D. Crimmins built numerous buildings, roads, and elevated lines, and published important volumes on many topics. Dennis Coghlin died in 1900 as a highly respected citizen of Toledo. William Harrity, after his term as chairman of the National Democratic Committee in 1892, returned to Philadelphia to build a respectable business career in a number of fields, including banking.

By the 1890's John Holland had built his Holland Boat Company into a thriving business and sold his submarines to various nations. In 1900 the first operational submarine in the United States Navy, the U.S.S. *Holland*, sailed from his shipyards. John W. Goff, one of

New York's great lawyers, exposed corruption in the 1890's and later served on the bench.[17] These and other accomplishments created for the Irish in America on the eve of World War I a world that in no way resembled the dark, bleak years of the 1850's. Nevertheless, the improvements in status did not cause the Irish-American to ignore the question of Ireland's freedom.

IV   *Return of the Irish Question*

For twenty years, Irish-American nationalism limped along with only occasional signs of healthy activity. The 1889 murder of Dr. Cronin discredited radicals, and the fall of Parnell forced the formation of a new organization in 1891 with a more conservative tone, the Irish National Federation of America, but Patrick Ford and other radicals bitterly condemned this effort. Ford and his kind hoped for a split between America and England and thought they had gained their illusive prize when President Cleveland threatened war with England over the Venezuelan issue of 1895. When war failed to materialize at that time and America under McKinley shifted to a policy of imperialism, Irish leaders bitterly complained that such a policy would lead to America's assumption of England's role in world affairs. Meanwhile, Anglo-American friendship grew. When rumors appeared toward the end of the 1890's that the two nations would sign an alliance, bitter Irish protest followed, but America's politicians and diplomats could now ignore the Irish. American policy continued to move toward imperialism and the end of Anglo-American animosity.[18]

One important reason for the failure of Irishmen in America to influence the nation's politics was the inability of Irish politicians to generate enough agitation in Ireland to create the cohesiveness the Irish in America experienced during the 1880's. Parnell's fall, the division of Irish politics, and the British concession on the land question—which removed it as an effective tool in nationalizing the people—combined to end agitation in Ireland. The Irish did attempt to create new ways to cultivate nationhood in these years in Douglas Hyde's Gaelic League, Sir Horace Plunkett's Irish Cooperative Movement, and Arthur Griffith's Sinn Fein party, but none of these accomplished that until a strange political twist forced the Liberals to seek the support of the Home Rule party on a budget question in 1910. John Redmond had, in effect, suddenly gained a position similar to Parnell's in the spring of 1886, the balance of power in Parliament. Suddenly, Home Rule was back in the air—the very issue that still stirred the hearts of the Irish in America.[19]

Meanwhile, conditions changed in America. Roosevelt's decision in 1908 not to run for reelection in effect gave the White House to William Howard Taft. The new president faced the difficult choice of supporting the policies of the Old Guard or the insurgent progressives who wanted a government more responsive to the needs of the people. Unfortunately, he blundered from one issue to the next until the insurgents led an open attack upon him and his policies at the close of 1909. Taft responded with an attempt to purge the latter from the party in the primary elections of 1910. That attempt failed, and the victorious insurgents moved to gain control of the party and keep the nomination for the presidency from Taft.

In the summer of that year Roosevelt returned from his African safari. His coolness toward President Taft and the administration's indifference to Roosevelt's efforts to reunite the Republicans only caused a wider divergence in the party. The off-year elections in November, 1910, gave the Democrats control of the House of Representatives for the first time since 1892 and a number of governorships in normally Republican states. The nation quite obviously had moved to the Left, and in the months that followed Roosevelt quickly emerged as the hope of Republican Progressives, while Taft became the hero of the regulars. This clear division led to a battle for the control of the Republican presidential nomination in 1912, and the split that resulted there gave the Democrats their greatest hope to capture the White House in twenty years. Fortunately for them, they found a candidate who could take advantage of the changing tone of the nation and the divisions among Republicans.

The arrival of Woodrow Wilson on the national scene and his capture of the Democratic presidential nomination, the success of Taft's forces in controlling the regular Republican convention, and Roosevelt's decision to run on a third-party label created a struggle which increased the significance of swing groups and led the various contestants to seek the foreign-born vote. In 1912, however, that element was a highly complex body of voters, over which the Irish had little control. Appeals to specific ethnic groups like the Italians or the Germans did not necessarily attract the Irish and vice versa.

Some regular Republicans made attempts to appeal directly to the Irish, but Roosevelt's Progressive party simply did not have an issue that would attract them, nor did they reveal much of a desire to become associated with the Irish. Wilson, meanwhile, made his appeals to the foreign-born but did not have to devote any special attention to the Irish, who were considered generally loyal to the Democratic party. Even Tammany entered Wilson's camp, delivering votes for him. The election itself turned on progressivism, an issue on which the Irish had little influence. Yet the election did mark the return of an era of division in American politics and created a situation in which, given the proper conditions, a well-organized minority group could control the necessary votes to swing an election. For the Irish this meant the possibility of using their power in America to aid Ireland's fight for freedom.[20]

CHAPTER 9

End of the Irish Struggle

I   *Hope in a German Victory*

ON the eve of World War I a series of events in Ireland again raised the possibility that Ireland would gain her freedom. In control of the balance of power in Parliament, John Redmond forced the Liberals to introduce a Home Rule Bill in exchange for his support of Liberal social reform. The Ulster Irish, who bitterly opposed any form of Home Rule, responded by creating a state within a state with its own government and army, the Ulster Volunteers. Irish nationalists in the South quickly answered with the National Volunteers, while the workers in Dublin formed a Citizen Army. Redmond, meanwhile, ignored the danger of violence as he awaited the passage of a Home Rule Bill. As the day approached in the spring and summer of 1914, both the "Ulsterites" and "Nationalists" armed their volunteers, but before violence could break out in Ireland, Europe exploded with the German attack on Belgium. Parliament then passed Home Rule with a clause that delayed its application until peace returned, but World War I changed the whole Irish Question long before the English could implement the act.[1]

The Irish in America watched these events carefully. Moderates cheered the leadership of John Redmond and the Home Rule Bill but had only words of disgust for the work of the Sinn Fein and those who sought violence. The *Irish World*, once a leading radical paper, supported this position, as did leading members of the church, including James Cardinal Gibbons. On the other hand, radicalism remained alive as John Devoy, an old revolutionary, and Daniel Cohalan, a New York Judge, at the head of a revived Clan-na-Gael called for independence, not Home Rule, and collected funds to arm and finance a revolution. The now somewhat militant Ancient Order of Hibernians, the largest Irish organization in the country, followed Devoy's leadership and, in convention after convention, demanded independence in preference to Home Rule.[2]

The events in the Anglo-Irish struggle that preceded World War I clearly failed to unify the Irish in America, but they did contribute to a renewed concern for things Irish. The language and literature of Ireland had attracted some attention in America before 1893, but the emergence of the Gaelic League as a vehicle of nationalism in Ireland soon stimulated a parallel development in America. The Ancient Order of Hibernians established a Chair of Gaelic Studies at Catholic University. Local Gaelic societies offered free instructions on Sundays. National conventions quickly followed as both William Butler Yeats and Padraic Pearse toured America with pleas to support the movement. Annual festivals emphasized not only the language, but Irish dancing, Gaelic songs, and essay contests on Irish history. Newspaper subscriptions again climbed, and movies, plays, lectures on Irish history, and books on Irish music carried the old stories and renewed the old awareness.[3]

In this atmosphere of new hope that Ireland would regain her freedom, in the revival of interest in things Irish, and in the return of the Democratic party to national power, it appeared that the Irish in America could once again use their power in American life to help Ireland, as they had done in the 1860's and 1880's. Then the war came. Within two years it changed the structure of Irish-American nationalism.

At first the moderate constitutionalists had little difficulty accepting Redmond's call to support England, especially in the light of the German attack on Belgium. The "lace curtain" Irish favored England for economic reasons, while many Irish-Americans had an attachment to France and therefore found themselves on England's side. All three groups readily accepted the propaganda pamphlet that Redmond and Sir Horace Plunkett wrote in support of the British war effort.

The revolutionaries, however, felt differently. For some time they had shown great interest in forming an alliance with the German-American community. The latter, reflecting the growing antagonism that characterized diplomatic relations between England and Germany in the first decade of the twentieth century, had grown somewhat anti-English during the late 1890's. The Irish noticed this tendency and the discovery of other mutual interests led to a conference of the national officers of the German Alliance and the Ancient Order of Hibernians in 1907, in which both groups agreed to fight Anglo-American friendship, restrictions on immigration, and other government policies. Irish-Americans marched in German parades, and Germans placed advertisements in Irish papers.

On the eve of World War I, the Clan-na-Gael and other Irish groups endorsed the 1907 pact. Devoy then used these connections to perfect his plan to use German power to guarantee the success of the revolt he had planned for Ireland. Along with Irish-born Jeremiah O'Leary, head of the American Truth Society, Devoy cultivated a friendship with leading German-Americans, made contact with the German embassy in Washington, later financed Roger Casement's 1914 trip to Germany to coordinate German support for the future revolution in Ireland, and published German propaganda in the pages of his *Gaelic-American*.[4]

In this way Irish-Americans supported diametrically opposed views as to the outcome of the war which naturally caused divisions over official American policy toward the conflict. Many, including leading Democratic politicians, such as Mayor Curley of Boston, supported President Wilson's policy of neutrality and his handling of the bitter disputes over neutral rights in 1914-15; yet a growing number of Irishmen denounced the president. The latter wanted America to grant Germany as much assistance as England and condemned Wilson for unfair practices under the guise of impartial neutrality. Suspecting him of using the laws to sell munitions only to England, they suggested an embargo on the munitions trade and an end to the sale of English and French bonds on the American market. The German sinking of the *Lusitania* caused these Irishmen to call for a law that would prevent travel by Americans on ships of belligerents.

Devoy and the radicals led these attacks at first; but, as time passed, more and more American Irishmen shifted their support to Germany. Wilson had never won much sympathy among the Irish, and in 1916 Devoy had little difficulty in organizing mass meetings in cities from coast to coast against the president's unneutral neutrality. These protests culminated in a great convention of the "Irish Race in America" in New York in March, 1916. Victor Herbert opened the meeting, and the twenty-three hundred delegates quickly asserted Ireland's claim to nationhood and demanded that America stay out of the war. Judges John W. Goff (who had prosecuted Croker's Tammany Hall in the 1890's) and Daniel F. Cohalan, as well as Devoy, addressed the delegates. That gathering unified the Irish in America, marked their reemergence as a pressure group at the national level, and organized them for their last effort to gain freedom for Ireland and for their own final acceptance by America.[5] At the same time, it marked the radicals as the spokesmen for the Irish in America.

The war had caused this shift from moderate to radical leadership in America, and it did so in Ireland as well. Redmond's support for England in 1914 matched the general enthusiasm of southern Ireland for the war as her sons quickly joined the ranks of the British army and soon died on the battlefields of France. By 1915, however, that enthusiasm had waned. The length of the war, its great slaughter, rising taxes, and the Liberal government's appointment of such men as Bonar Law and Edward Carson, the Ulster firebrand, to the cabinet combined to generate increasing apathy. Furthermore, the National Volunteers split over Redmond's pledge that they would fight for England, and on September 30, 1914 about ten thousand resigned from the larger body to form the Irish Volunteers. These men accepted the leadership of the Irish Revolutionary Brotherhood, which received funds from America. By November they had joined forces with the workers of Dublin and prepared for the revolution that Devoy had dreamed about for years.

Roger Casement, the Irish nationalist, meanwhile, with money gathered in America, arrived in Germany and asked for military support of a revolution in Ireland. The German lack of enthusiasm convinced Casement that the Irish Revolutionary Brotherhood should cancel the revolution, but Devoy refused. On Easter Monday the insurgents marched through the streets of Dublin. They quickly seized a number of buildings, but no uprising occurred in the country. The flag of the Irish Republic flew in the breeze of Dublin's sky for only six days. The British army quickly suppressed the revolt and captured its leaders.[6]

The Easter Rebellion, as it was soon called, fired Irish-American emotions to new heights as the British executed the fifteen leaders as well as Casement without civil trial. Americans in general responded with expressions of outrage, while Irish-Americans offered masses for their souls; Cardinals of the church appealed for the relief of the victims of Ireland's Easter week; public meetings denounced the stupidity of the British, and Senator William E. Borah condemned the executions on the floor of the Senate.

In the midst of this excitement, Wilson received the Democratic presidential nomination for a second time. In the campaign that followed, both parties showed a major interest in the Irish vote. The Irish radicals condemned Wilson for his many slurs about disloyal hyphenates, and they openly campaigned against him. The Republican candidate, Charles Evans Hughes, actually met with the Irish-American, Jeremiah O'Leary. Afterward, O'Leary wrote an insulting letter to Wilson, who responded by saying he did not need the support of the disloyal. In spite of this opposition, many of the professional Irish politicians supported Wilson. On the surface, Charles Murphy and his Tammany "braves" pledged their support to Wilson, but, when the votes were counted, Wilson carried New York City by only forty thousand, not enough to offset the upstate Republican lead. Hughes carried New York, but Wilson won California and the election. He owed the Irish nothing, and when the time came to pay his political debts, he gave them just that. [7]

The election did not discourage Devoy in his belief that a German victory would lead to Ireland's independence, but now, more than ever, he had to keep America out of the war. When the president took steps against Germany in early 1917, Devoy condemned him and gave high praise to those senators who blocked the president's request to arm America's merchant marine.

When Wilson finally asked for war on April 2, Irish leaders flooded Congress with appeals against any declaration of war, but again they failed. Congress passed the president's request, and any Irish plan to use Germany's power to gain Irish freedom immediately evaporated. [8]

II   Struggle to Reach Wilson

The new situation caused problems for many Irish-Americans. They could no longer support an enemy, but they found it most difficult to say anything nice about an established ally. Devoy's verbal attacks upon England continued and, in effect, caused many Americans to question the loyalty of all Irishmen in America. Irish-Americans quickly denounced radicals who tainted them with treason, but Devoy and his friends denied their anti-British feelings meant they were un-American. Meanwhile, other Irish-Americans quickly joined the army and added to the military legends of the past. The famous "Fighting Sixty-ninth" New York Regiment arrived in France with the first American troops and immediately built an enviable reputation. Church leaders supported the war effort, and Irishmen called attention to their patriotism whenever they could.[9]

In short, the Irish in America spent the first year of the war proving their Americanism—a situation which generated a great deal of despair among those who wanted a free Ireland. On January 8, 1918, President Wilson offered these Irish-Americans a ray of hope. In an address before a joint session of Congress the president explained to the world the nation's war aims. "What we demand in this war, therefore, is nothing particular to ourselves. It is that the world be made fit and safe to live in; and particularly that it be made safe for every peace-loving nation which, like our own, wishes to live its own life, determine its own institutions, be assured of justice and fair dealing by the other peoples of the world as against force and selfish aggression." He then enumerated the famous Fourteen Points and concluded with "the one principle that ran through the whole program. It is the principle of justice to all peoples of all nationalities and their right to live on equal terms of liberty and safety with one another whether they be strong or weak."[10]

Many Americans received those words as a sign of a new world that would emerge from the ashes of war, but the Irish reaction varied. Some believed Wilson had accepted Ireland's claim to determine her own destiny, but others questioned why he had not specifically included her among those oppressed countries that would receive their liberty and autonomy. All applauded the concept of self-determination, but they also condemned any attempt to exclude Ireland from the list of countries to receive those rights.

Coming as it did after the great excitement of 1916 and the relative calm of 1917, Wilson's speech changed the whole tenor of life for the Irish in America. With no hope for revolution in Ireland and no hope for salvation in a German victory, Irish aspirations had no place to go in search of aid until Wilson spoke. His words led them back to the older idea, to use their power in America to force the United States to intervene in the Anglo-Irish struggle on the side of Ireland. To accomplish that, however, the Irish knew they had to convince the policy-makers to guarantee Ireland's inclusion in the peace plans, and that meant direct pressure.

It started immediately. On January 11 the president received Mrs. Hannah Sheehy-Skeffington, widow of the martyred Irish pacifist, who presented him with an urgent plea from the Irish Women's Council of Dublin that the United States recognize the existence of the republic. On the same day, a delegation of Irish-Americans led by Senator James D. Phelan of California, a close political associate of Wilson and one of his staunch defenders in the Senate, presented him with a statue of Robert Emmett, the nineteenth-century Irish revolutionary martyr. Phelan's prepared statement earnestly implored Wilson to actively support the freedom of Ireland. A week later, Éamon De Valéra, a survivor of the Easter Rebellion, while demanding that the great powers recognize Ireland as a separate state with no ties to England, spoke directly to Wilson: "We say that if those who go about mouthing of an independent Irish state do not take that interpretation of it, they are hypocrites, and we tell President Wilson, in view of the statements he has made, if he does not take that view of it, he is as big a hypocrite as Lloyd George."[11]

The Irish also applied pressure to Congress. By February, a number of representatives had offered various resolutions, all of which in one way or another asked for American support of Ireland's claim to freedom. When the chairman of the House Foreign Affairs Committee failed to push these resolutions to the floor of the House, the leaders of sixteen Irish-American organizations sent him a joint letter asking that the committee act upon these resolutions immediately. But nothing came of such demands; many felt it would not be in the public interest to grant such a request as it might be construed as an interference in the internal affairs of a friendly nation.

At the same time, Judge Cohalan and the Friends of Irish Freedom in conjunction with other organizations began to generate public support through mass meetings. Hardly an issue of any Irish-American newspaper appeared without mention of such meetings. In towns across the country during Easter week of 1918, these meetings ended in the passage of resolutions demanding that the United States support the independence of Ireland. This culminated on May 18 when Irishmen gathered in New York for the Second Irish Race Convention. At this gathering, Justice John Goff presented a resolution which called for "the application to Ireland, now, of President Wilson's noble declaration of the right of every people to self-rule and self-determination" and specifically asked Wilson to "exert every legitimate and friendly influence in favor of self-determination for the people of Ireland."[12]

Wilson, meanwhile, "was determined not to embarrass the British government by suggesting a settlement of the Irish Question," yet in the summer and early fall of 1918, his words and actions actually increased Irish-American hopes for eventual success. By September one Irish editor declared that "President Wilson made it clear in his New York speech that Ireland was included among the list of peoples and nations which must be made free as a result of this great war." Even John Devoy declared, "Wilson is for self-determination for all people."[13]

The question of American support of Ireland's claim to self-determination naturally entered the congressional campaign in the fall of 1918. In Pennsylvania, for instance, the local branches of the Friends of Irish Freedom asked all candidates for major office: "will you, if elected to the public office for which you are a candidate, openly and unequivocally support Ireland's claims to complete independence, the form of government to be determined by the whole male and female population of Ireland?" Eight Republican and Democratic congressional candidates, and the two candidates for governor, endorsed this statement on the front pages of the Philadelphia *Irish Press*. At the same time, Devoy urged his readers to support the Democrats as the surest way of achieving Ireland's freedom.[14]

While the politicians debated this question, mass meetings continued, and petitions were passed. Letters came from the citizens of Butte, Montana, the Executive Board of the Clan-na-Gael, the Irish Progressive League, citizens of Cleveland, the New York Central Federated Union, and the Friendly Sons of Saint Patrick. The clergy of Philadelphia, San Francisco, New York, Chicago, Saint Louis, Newark, Boston, Catholic University in Washington, D.C., and the bishops of the province of Pennsylvania sent similar letters. The tempo of the mass meetings increased, especially after the signing of the Armistice, reaching a climax during the week of December 8-15, 1918, which was designated "Self-Determination Week." A huge gathering met in Madison Square Garden on December 10 to hear William Cardinal O'Connell of Boston declare: "This war we are told again and again [is] . . . for the inalienable right, inherent in every nation, of self-determination. The war can be justified only by the universal application of those principles. Let that application begin with Ireland."

The meeting ended with the passage of a resolution which Wilson received as he sailed across the Atlantic to attend the peace conference. It "urged him to demand . . . self-determination for the people of Ireland." Similar meetings in Chicago; Philadelphia; Denver; Baltimore; Louisville; Portland; New Haven; Omaha; Buffalo; Seattle; New Orleans; Manchester; San Francisco; Brockton, Massachusetts; and Chester, Pennsylvania ended in similar resolutions. This mounting pressure prompted Wilson to promise "he would do his utmost to bring about a just and satisfactory solution to a delicate problem."[15]

The Paris Peace Conference opened in January, 1919, only to find the Irish problem more complex than ever. The Easter Rebellion and the executions that followed completely discredited the Home Rule party and boosted the appeal of the Sinn Fein, so much so that in the British parliamentary elections of December, 1918, the latter party won seventy-three seats. These newly elected representatives refused to go to London, met in Dublin on January 7, 1919, and organized a constituent assembly for Ireland. Two weeks later, they adopted a constitution, issued a Declaration of Irish independence, and authorized a delegation to travel to Paris to represent Ireland at the Paris Peace Conference.[16] Consequently, Wilson and his fellow statesmen found an independent nation pounding on their Paris doors, not an oppressed majority.

These events further unified the Irish in America and strengthened their demands for self-determination as to the solution to the Irish Question. Since the people of Ireland had, in effect, exercised that right in the December elections, they argued that simple recognition of the Irish Republic would end the Irish Question. Many realized England's reluctance to accept that solution, and they argued that the statesmen at Paris could solve the problem by recognizing Ireland's right to self-determination, thus forcing England into granting it. In their view, the decision of the president of the United States carried paramount weight, and Irish leaders decided to arouse public opinion in order to force Wilson into presenting the representatives of the Irish people to the peace conference.

The Third Irish Race Convention convened in Philadelphia on

February 20, 1919 in that atmosphere. Over five thousand delegates arrived in time to hear Cardinal Gibbons declare, "all Americans should stand as one man for Ireland's inalienable right of self-determination." The delegates wildly cheered for a resolution which called upon "the Paris Peace Conference to apply to Ireland the great doctrine of national self-determination." Wilson was in the United States at this time, and a special committee presented this resolution to him, but the president avoided any clear promise to raise Ireland's right to self-determination at the peace conference or to ask the conference to give the Irish delegates an opportunity to present their case.[17]

Meanwhile, the Irish were successful in other political quarters. The governor of Missouri "strongly favored self-determination for Ireland," and legislative bodies in Pennsylvania, Missouri, Colorado, and California passed resolutions with similar calls. The Committee on Foreign Affairs of the House of Representatives discussed a number of these resolutions and in late January focused attention upon one introduced by Representative Thomas Gallagher of Illinois. The administration wanted the committee to delay action on this resolution, but this proved useless as both sides played with it to get the Irish vote. Wilson intervened personally and ordered his private secretary, Joseph Tumulty, to explain to congressional leaders that he feared the Gallagher resolution would disrupt Anglo-American relations. This pressure, in addition to the misgivings of at least the committee chairman, caused the committee to report a weak substitute, which Congress debated on the last day of the session, March 3, 1919.

The debate itself lasted for about three hours and carried into the late evening with Democrats and Republicans accusing each other of not having sufficient love for Ireland. The resolution finally passed, 216 to 45, in the closing minutes of the session, but the Senate, fortunately, had no time to consider the resolution, and thus it had no legal force upon Wilson. Yet even if time had permitted, the Senate most probably would not have approved the action of the House. A similar resolution, introduced by Senator Phelan, had already gathered dust for months, as his colleagues had refused to consider it. Irish political power quite obviously could force the issue into the halls of Congress but could not force Congress to pass any strong resolution that would bind the president's hands.[18]

This action of a Democratic Congress did not mean that Democrats in general took the Irish for granted. On the contrary, as the mass meetings continued, they became more concerned than ever. On March 28 a number of Democratic senators sent a letter to Wilson in which they called:

attention to the necessity of seeing that some progress is made before the Peace Conference adjourns toward a solution of the vexing question of self-determination for Ireland. It is not alone that the future of our party imperatively demands that something be done before the work of the peace conference comes to an end to meet the reasonable expectations of the Irish people, but we will all concur in the view that the prospect of early ratification of the treaty by the Senate will be jeopardized otherwise.[19]

In April the Irish went directly to Wilson for a second time in three months. The Third Irish Race Convention had formed an American Commission for Irish Independence to represent the Irish in America at the peace conference and to do all in its power to convince the statesmen of the world that Ireland should be free. On April 17 Wilson met the commission's chairman, Frank P. Walsh, who asked him to intervene on behalf of the Irish representatives. The president informed Walsh that "it is not within the province of the American delegation to request the Peace Conference to receive a delegation composed of citizens of a country other than our own," but he did later ask the British unofficially if they would permit De Valéra's party to come to Paris. In May, however, Walsh and his fellow commissioners toured Ireland where they delivered a number of speeches. Wilson claimed that the wild nature of these speeches destroyed any hope of a British agreement on this point.[20]

Meanwhile, on May 7, 1919, the conference released a treaty draft which did not mention Ireland. Appalled and embittered, the Irish in America immediately condemned Wilson. Seeing the political possibilities in their reaction, Senator William Borah introduced a resolution in the Senate: "that the Senate of the United States earnestly request the American Peace Commission at Versailles to secure, if possible, for the representatives chosen by the people of Ireland . . . a hearing before said Peace Conference in order that said representatives may present the case of Ireland and ask international recognition of the government, republican in form, established by the people of Ireland."

On June 5, the Senate's Foreign Affairs Committee reported a somewhat weaker version: "that the Senate of the United States earnestly requests the American Commission at Versailles to endeavor to secure for Éamon De Valéra, Arthur Griffith and Count George Noble Plunkett a hearing before said Peace Conference in order that they may present the case of Ireland." It passed, 60 to 1. Senator Thomas Walsh later condemned the Senate for approving Borah's resolution for "political purposes only," and he immediately received a storm of protest letters. One of these adequately forecasted the plight of the party:

The Irish people in the North are the backbone of the Democratic Party in many states. Senator Phelan can tell you that the almost solid vote they gave the President in San Francisco saved the election in 1916. Members of the Democratic National Committee . . . and others are fearful that the *failure* of the Irish Question may lose us much of our remaining members of the party in the North. The only place where we made any gains last fall were in the districts heavily populated by the Irish. I wonder if you have given any consideration to the thought that such an attack as you have delivered against the Irish people may not result in further destruction of the party. . . . The sooner that the Democratic Party encourages and supports the aspirations of the Irish race, the better for its safety and promotion; for without the support of the Irish people, our party will remain in a hapless minority for a long time to come.

Senator Borah admitted the political motivation but he "defended the action of the Senate by declaring that Ireland should have received the same treatment afforded other oppressed peoples."[21]

This debate, however, came too late. The Paris Peace Conference had completed its final work without offering any help to Ireland in her struggle for independence. With that knowledge, Wilson had to face Frank P. Walsh for a final meeting. In a remarkable statement the president intimated that he might have made a mistake with the whole self-determination proposal:

You have touched the great metaphysical tragedy of today. When I gave utterance to those words, I said them without knowledge that nationalities existed which are coming to us day after day. Of course, Ireland's case from the point of population, from the point of view of the struggle it has made, from the point of interest it has excited in the world and especially among our people, whom I am anxious to serve, is the outstanding case of a small nationality. You do not know and you can not appreciate the anxieties I have experienced as the result of these millions of people having their hopes raised by what I have said.[22]

Wilson also admitted that he did not permit the Irish issue to rise to the surface of the discussions because he feared it would destroy Anglo-American unity. He needed to guarantee the success of the League of Nations, which he hoped would eventually find solutions to the many requests for aid.

For eighteen months, the Irish in America with great confidence had placed their hopes in Wilson's hands only to learn in June that he had failed to deliver. Never before had they placed so much belief in such a sure thing; never before had they come so close. That height of expectation was smashed, and a profound bitterness followed. The Irish quickly found their scapegoats—Wilson, his treaty, and his League. For the next eighteen months they worked with the same ferocious vigor that had characterized the previous eighteen months—to destroy all three.

III   *Struggle to Kill the Treaty and the League*

The reaction began shortly after the text was released. On May 24 one Irish editorial declared, "If the League of Nations goes into effect as now presented, Americans will be bound to assist England in crushing any insurrection that might occur in Ireland." On June 1 Senator Borah in a letter read at an Irish-American meeting in Oregon, stated that Article 10 would continue the subjugation of Ireland since it would force Americans to guarantee boundaries by the conference.[23] By freezing the status quo, it would guarantee that Ireland would remain under the paw of "the British Lion."

Similar arguments appeared in the Senate in the midst of the debate on Borah's Irish resolution. Senator Albert B. Fall declared that "if a revolution arose in Ireland, or in any other nation, it would become the duty of the League of Nations to send assistance to put down that revolution, exactly as France acted as mandatory and as Austria acted as mandatory for the Holy Alliance in 1822 and 1823." Senator Phelan immediately challenged this argument and claimed that Article 10 was expressly limited to external attack. Before he could sit down, however, Senator Vance McCormick argued that, according to Article 3, "the assembly may deal at its gatherings with any matter within the sphere of action of the League affecting the peace of the world." Phelan immediately denied that a revolution in Ireland would come within the sphere of the action of the League or disturb the peace of the world and that to try to extend the clause on "external aggression" to cover internal revolt was utterly ridiculous. McCormick had a rebuttal, however, and declared that the president had stated "under the League, armed forces would intervene to protect the right of national minorities." If the League had this power, it obviously would have the power to intervene in local revolutions. To this, Phelan offered no comment.[24]

While Congress debated the issue, the Friends of Irish Freedom began to use their million-dollar Victory Fund to defeat the League. They distributed over 1,300,000 pamphlets, published full and half-page ads in newspapers across the country, and issued full-page rebuttals of the president's speeches in the newspapers of the various towns in which he spoke during his famous tour in defense of his ideas.[25]

To complicate matters further for Wilson, Éamon De Valéra arrived in the United States on June 25 and immediately began a whirlwind tour that lasted for months and took him to every corner of the United States. Wherever he went, officials received him with open arms. Every edition of an Irish-American newspaper carried an article concerning his visits and his receptions. His continued appearances and inflammatory speech-making fueled Irish tempers to a fever pitch.

These activities increased the number of mass meetings, the number of resolutions passed, and the number of petitions sent to Congress; the question clearly became American as well as Irish-American. The American Federation of Labor, meeting in its national convention, called for congressional recognition of the Irish Republic. The City Council of Cincinnati and numerous state legislatures demanded Irish freedom. The Democratic Committee of Massachusetts and the Annual Democratic Convention of New Jersey condemned the League's covenant and England's attempts to deny Ireland her freedom.[27] It appeared as if the entire force of American opinion was converging upon the Senate of the United States.

Wilson's friends in the Senate met this onslaught with various explanations of how circumstances forced the exclusion of Ireland from the list of American war aims, and how the League of Nations would aid Ireland in her struggle "because it would embarrass the

British into giving self-determination to her." Senator Borah dismissed that hope as rubbish and declared that the treaty would never help Ireland recover her independence because she could not revolt successfully without outside aid and that any third nation that supported an Irish revolution, even America, would be obligated to England under Article 10. If this happened, Irish-Americans, in effect, would suppress an Irish revolution. Senator Thomas Walsh of Montana accused Borah of "a studied effort, usually insidious, but not infrequently direct to arouse the prejudice of our citizens of Irish birth or descent against the League."[28] Unfortunately for Wilson and his friends, that was all too true and all too successful.

The pressure generated by Irish-Americans finally forced the Democrats in the Senate to offer a resolution which asked that the United States government present to the League of Nations the Irish Question "and the right of its people to self-government." Henry Cabot Lodge saw this as "an attempt to save the League,"[29] and many Irish-Americans agreed. Nevertheless, it failed, for on November 19, 1919, the United States Senate rejected Wilson's dream.

The role the Irish played in its defeat is hard to assess. Before the vote Senator Walsh of Montana believed that passage or rejection would depend largely upon the possession of the Irish vote, and after its defeat Senator Borah immediately telegramed Judge Cohalan: "greatest victory for country since revolution, largely due to you."[30]

IV   Last Battle

The defeat of the League caused the Irish in America to shift their interests once again to the solution of Ireland's immediate problems which by the fall of 1919 had become increasingly complex. The Sinn Fein victory in the December, 1918, elections and subsequent party actions quickly led to a state within a state with its own courts, taxes, and a regular army. The British reacted with a policy of suppression. In March, 1920, they introduced the famous Black and Tans, a police force of hastily recruited unemployed veterans of the world war. Many were shell-shocked, and a few had a prison record. In July the government added the Auxiliaries, an elite force of ex-officers. A brutal guerrilla war followed, with the Irish Republican Army under Michael Collins attacking the various military and police forces on the island, while the Black and Tans retaliated with attacks upon civilians as well as upon members of the Irish Republican Army.[31]

The outrages committed by British forces in Ireland in the name of England infuriated the Irish in America and caused them to organize numerous relief agencies, but they could do little to force official American involvement. However, they did make one final effort. Representative William F. Mason, a Republican from Illinois, had introduced a bill in May, 1919, to provide $14,000 for the establishment of a diplomatic mission in Ireland, and in late November, 1919, the Irish demanded its passage. The House Foreign Affairs Committee held hearings on the bill in the next month, but the committee refused to release it in spite of constant demands by Irish editors for its approval during the early months of 1920.[32]

In the midst of this pressure, Wilson's followers sought to have the Senate reconsider the question of the treaty and the League. In an effort to placate the Irish, Senator Peter Gerry of Rhode Island offered a fifteenth reservation to the treaty: "In consenting to the ratification of the treaty with Germany, the United States addresses to the principle of self-determination and to the resolutions of sympathy with the aspirations of the Irish people for a government of their own choice, adopted by the Senate on June 6, 1919, and declares that when self-government is attained by Ireland, a consummation it is hoped is at hand, it should promptly be admitted as a member of the League of Nations."[33] The Senate accepted this resolution in a close vote on March 18, 36 to 30, but two days later rejected the treaty for a second time.

This last defeat of the treaty caused the Irish again to pressure for passage of the Mason bill, which continued to linger in committee. Finally, on May 27 the committee reported a substitute resolution which linked the statement of sympathy for the Irish cause to the general American sympathy for all oppressed nationalities and claimed that the conditions generated by the Black and Tans in Ireland threatened world peace. Americans wanted a settlement in order to avoid war and because the whole question threatened British-American friendship, which the nation could not afford. Mason called upon the House to issue this statement of sympathy "with the aspirations of the Irish people for a government of their own choice," but the resolution never came to a vote.[34] Once again events proved that the Irish could force an issue onto the floor of Congress, but they could not force its passage.

By this time the presidential campaign of 1920 had started, and Wilson wanted to make the election a solemn referendum on his peace settlement and the league. In that context he wrote off the Irish. De Valéra, still in the United States, then went to Chicago for the Republican Convention to pressure that party into writing an Irish plank into their platform. Judge Cohalan also attended that meeting, but neither had much success with the convention managers. By this time, De Valéra and Cohalan had split on what was best for Ireland, and their open division weakened Ireland's case. No Irish plank appeared in the Republican platform. They did nominate Warren G. Harding for the presidency, however, and he immediately gained the support of many Irish editors who urged readers to vote for anyone but the Democratic candidate. John Devoy went as far as to ask his readers to vote against Al Smith, the New York gubernatorial candidate, because he favored the League of Nations.

The Democrats nominated James M. Cox of Ohio and fought hard to hold the Irish vote, but the revolt against Wilson and his League proved all too real. Cox suffered an overwhelming defeat, and the defection of Irish voters in the large cities contributed to the outcome. In his natural way Devoy claimed credit for the defeat of the Democrats, and Cox later stated that "the professional Irish" had mustered enough votes to defeat him. Whether this was true or not made little difference to the Irish, as they obviously enjoyed the success of their effort to destroy the League.[35] In the immediate aftermath, few realized they had witnessed the last such expression of Irish power at a national level. Events in Ireland soon destroyed the one issue around which all Irish-Americans could rally.

While the Irish in America fought to defeat Wilson's dream, their cousins in Ireland fought to stay alive. The British policy of reprisals had created a reign of terror which touched upon every corner of the island. "Bloody Sunday," November 21, 1920, saw both sides murder each other in Dublin, while December brought news of successful Irish Republican Army attacks upon the hated Auxies, the short title of the Auxiliaries. Black and Tan reprisals against the people of Cork followed. World public opinion began to condemn these acts by established agents of the British government, while Americans organized the American Commission on Conditions in Ireland. This body held hearings through January, 1921 and issued a final report that condemned the Irish Republican Army; but it had stronger words of condemnation for the British forces in Ireland. Opinion continued to shift through the spring of 1921, and by the early summer the British decided to end the struggle. At noon on July 11 hostilities ceased. The battle was over, and Ireland, in effect, had gained her freedom. De Valéra later refused to accept the terms of the final treaty which led to a bitter civil war that lasted from June, 1922, to April, 1923, but these events had little real effect upon the Irish in America. United during the Black and Tan terror, they divided over the civil war and quickly became disgusted with the turn of events. Then, in 1923, John Devoy died. His funeral in Dublin appropriately closed an era in the American-Irish-English triangle that began in the 1860's.[36]

CHAPTER 10

Irish as Americans

I *Impact of Fewer Immigrants*

T HE Irish migration to America continued in the years that
followed 1923, but the numbers fell considerably. The more
settled political conditions in Ireland that followed independence
removed an important cause of migration; yet economic conditions
did not improve to any appreciable extent under the new
government, and large numbers continued to leave the island.
However, all did not come to America. The immigration restriction
legislation of the 1920's discouraged newcomers in general, and
although it was not directed against the Irish, it did change
America's image as a haven of the poor. The depression and World
War II further broke the old patterns of movement to America, and
in the period since 1945 most of those who left the island went to
England's industry or to other parts of the once powerful British
Empire. Thus, in the 1950's and 1960's the number of Irish
newcomers continued to decline until today, as a result of new
restrictions, there is little more than a trickle. [1]

This decline in numbers, coupled with other changes in the
American Irish community, had a profound effect upon those who
chose to emigrate to America. Their ancestors had arrived in such
numbers in such a short period of time that they seemed to threaten
the existence of Protestant America, but in the fifty years since
Ireland gained her independence, Americans have found such
threats in groups other than the Irish. After a hundred years the
Irish had lost their visibility.

Simultaneously, changing patterns in American housing created a
world far removed from that of the 1850's. World War I started a
great internal migration in America. The Negro moved from the
static agrarian life in the South to the more dynamic industrial
society of the northern cities. His arrival in large numbers changed
the pattern of life in America's cities and accelerated the process

that caused the Irish to move to the edge of the cities and eventually into the suburbs. Those ethnic groups that arrived in the twenty years before World War I had started the process that led to the dispersion of the Irish, but in the 1920's whole neighborhoods moved. Where before 1910 the Irish maintained a Saint Patrick's church in central Philadelphia, they moved to parishes like Saint Francis and the Most Blessed Sacrament churches in west Philadelphia in the 1920's and 1930's and then into the suburban parishes of Delaware County in the 1940's and 1950's. The Irish sections of Germantown in northwest Philadelphia gave way to the Negro's drive for decent housing only in the 1960's, and the Irish who moved found new homes in the scattered northwestern suburbs. A similar pattern has occurred in other cities and the strength of that movement does not appear to be weakening.

This change in living patterns had its effect upon the newly arrived Irish. In the 1920's and 1930's they either found homes in the new "Irish towns" on the edge of the city or simply faded into the suburbs. Scattered in this way and living in clean, respectable neighborhoods of private homes, they became less conspicuous than ever.[2]

At the same time, the very causes of their migration permitted them to fade further into American society. Before 1920 the Irish emigrated to America as a result of a combination of religious, national, and economic reasons and blamed their problems upon the hated English. Through much of the nineteenth century open prejudice greeted their arrival, and in that situation they found security in the familiar world in numbers. After 1920 they came for purely economic reasons. Ireland simply could not provide them with a means to make a living. They came without hating anyone, or anything, and found little prejudice to greet them. Because of the reputation and positions of power earned by their predecessors they were guaranteed acceptance. In effect, they could live anywhere as long as they had the means, and they no longer had to start and stop at the very bottom of the economic scale. They saw no signs reading "Irish need not apply"; only in the upper echelons of the professional levels of American life did the Irish-Catholic encounter any significant degree of prejudice.[3]

In the years since World War II more and more have moved into the middle class. They own their homes; many have two cars; and most of them can afford annual vacations. They still fill the ranks of

America's law enforcement agencies, but many others have become teachers, lawyers, and doctors. Irishmen fill positions at all levels of business and government. All of this made the path for the newer immigrants easier as they now blended with the middle class with relative ease. Today, in the early 1970's, they are scattered throughout white middle-class suburbs.[4] The focus is no longer on them.

During these years the new immigrants did make serious attempts to maintain the old traditions. For years they listened to Irish music and news on radio stations in America's large cities. Local associations devoted to the preservation of Irish history and other Irish traditions existed in many areas. Essay contests on topics from the past and demonstrations of traditional dancing attracted the attention of the Irish community. Gaelic football games were played into the 1960's, but in all of these activities interest continued to wane; the second generation had little time for these things. Only a declining first generation gave attention to such pastimes, but even here the interest was not overwhelming. These men and women wanted to become Americans, and as long as no pressure existed to remain Irish they tended to forget the past.[5]

Some remnants of the once prolific Irish press lingered into the post-World War II years, but these carried only the news from Ireland which had little appeal to anyone but the first generation. Even there the news was generally local gossip; seldom did the great important issues that once filled the columns of Patrick Ford's *Irish World* appear. The end of the nationalist struggle with England killed any necessity for the radical press of a John Devoy, and when he died in 1923, his paper died with him. Even the once mighty role of the Irish-American press to Americanize the newcomer disappeared as the Irish increased the ranks of the middle class. Today, what Irish press remains is of an antiquarian nature. Even the great Catholic press of the nineteenth century which placed such great stress upon Irish affairs had lost that characteristic by the 1930's. Other problems, more Catholic and American in nature, filled their columns, and only historians paid any attention to the old issues.[6]

The younger immigrants continued to patronize Irish dances well into the 1950's and there met their future husbands and wives, but the intermarriage rate continued to climb. As they moved into the suburbs, they met other partners. They continued to find Catholic mates, for the most part, but the Irish-marrying-Irish syndrome gave way to unions with Germans, Italians, and Poles. This was especially true among the second generation and among those who had gone to college.

The once mighty Ancient Order of Hibernians gradually became nothing more than a private club where one could buy beer on Sunday at reasonable rates. As the Irish moved from the old neighborhoods, the clubhouses gradually deteriorated until today some limp along without any visible sign that the Irish once owned that part of the city.[7]

The great fund drives of the past to support elections of Irish-Catholics to Parliament or the destruction of the London Bridge have given away to benefit dances, the proceeds from which would be given to a visiting priest from Ireland who would use the money to build a new church either at home (Ireland) or in some missionary land. The once powerful benevolent societies gradually lost their purpose as the Irish gained a degree of financial stability and the New Deal transferred the burden of caring for the poor from the private to the public sector. Benefit dances continued for individual families suddenly found in want, but even these declined in numbers during the 1950's and 1960's.[8]

As these changes came to the Irish, they also lived through the frustrations of American life, and a number of myths concerning their reactions to those problems persist. The Depression, for instance, created two personalities that captured the two themes of the Irish-Catholic community. Father Charles Coughlin, a Catholic priest who spoke to America from a radio station in his church, the Shrine of the Little Flower in Royal Oak, Michigan, first limited himself to religious issues, but by 1930 he had entered the political arena and urged direct government action to offset the effects of the Depression. Later he offered simplistic causes and solutions to the problems of the times. Soon he saw the bankers as criminals against mankind, and before long he was attacking Roosevelt, Communists, and Jews. How many Irish listened to him is difficult to say, but a substantial number of those who had just reached some degree of respectability and economic stability on the eve of the Depression did. He voiced their fears and offered solutions they could understand. More important, he touched upon that one curse of mankind so often heard in the conversations at the now declining AOH clubs—the Jew. Fortunately, Father Coughlin's excesses killed his appeal, but some Irish-Catholics still believe that his attacks upon the Jews led to his downfall, that the American Jewish community demanded that the Bishops silence him, and that they did.[9]

On the other side, if Coughlin spoke to one group of Irish-Catholics, his leading clerical critic, an Irish-Catholic, spoke to the other side. Msgr. John Ryan, born on a midwestern farm in 1869 of parents that had emigrated from Tipperary in 1859, had often heard Ignatius Donnelly lecture the legislators of Minnesota on the necessity of passing the social legislation that the farmers and workers of America needed. From that and the experience of his own life, he naturally sought a career that would harmonize religion and economics. In 1906 his book, *A Living Wage*, proposed certain principles that eventually reached reality in the New Deal legislation of the 1930's. For the next thirty years he worked for his beliefs of social reform, and when Coughlin condemned Roosevelt's economic policies, Ryan responded with a solid counterattack that appealed to the liberal side of the Irish-Catholic community.[10]

In the years after World War I, the Catholic church remained for the most part safely in the hands of the Irish clergy. Many of the old leaders died as the war came to a close, but a new generation took their place. William O'Connell continued as archbishop and cardinal of Boston, while Dennis Dougherty presided in Philadelphia as archbishop and later as cardinal. Patrick J. Hayes received the post in New York and one could find priests named Kelly in Grand Rapids, Gallagher in Detroit, Walsh in Trenton, and Shaw in New Orleans. When James Cardinal Gibbons died in 1921, a Curley took his place. The lower ranks of the clergy reflected the dream of the Irish-Catholic mother to have a son a priest and a daughter in the convent.

For the individual Irish-Catholic, the church continued to influence his life, but some changes appeared. Family recitation of the rosary and other prayers lost some significance as the church started to emphasize parish activities. The papal decrees on early First Communion and frequent or daily communion caused this shift, as did a whole series of new devotions that developed in the aftermath of the war. The desire for Catholic education actually grew with the capacity of the church to maintain and expand its school system. The Irish child literally lived in a world of religion, and none of the authoritarianism of the past had disappeared.

If the church continued to influence the Irish, the Irish were not as successful in continuing their control of the church. The influx of immigrants from Eastern and Southern Europe had reopened the demands for national-language churches, and sons of these newcomers soon discovered that the Catholic church could serve them as a way out of the ghetto, as it had done for the Irish. New leaders thus slowly appeared in church councils. Although John O'Hara followed Dennis Dougherty as archbishop of Philadelphia in 1952, he did not pass his office to a fellow Irishman when he died in 1960. John Krol, a Polish-American, came to Philadelphia to rule a church where only the Irish had ruled before. A more startling change came ten years later when William O'Connell's successor in Boston, the Irish-American Richard Cardinal Cushing, resigned. The pope appointed to that most Irish of American sees a Portuguese American, Humberto S. Medeiros. On October 7, 1970, the new archbishop took his office, and four weeks later Cardinal Cushing died. An era in American church history had ended.[11]

If these changes in church leadership indicated what had happened to the Irish in America in the fifty years since World War I, one can find other changes in other aspects of life. The Irish in America had produced a number of educated men in the nineteenth century, but as a group they paid little attention to education, especially higher education. They supported their parish schools and the Catholic high schools that appeared early in the twentieth century, but they did so more to defend the faith than to foster a love of learning in their children. The great mass of Irishmen had little time for books; only the "lace curtain" Irish had any interest in sending their children to college. The Irish moneyed class seldom supported intellectual research, and this failure guaranteed that the American Irish Historical Society would never really compete with the American Jewish Historical Society.

All this began to change in the 1920's as enrollments in Catholic institutions of higher learning increased. The Depression quickly put a stop to this development, and World War II delayed its revival. When the war ended, however, the GI Bill suddenly provided an opportunity for thousands to go to college. As these men graduated in the early 1950's, the Irish discovered what American Jews had known for some time—education paved the way out of the ghetto and up the ladder of American society. Those who came to America in the 1920's and 1930's had children ready for college, and these second-generation Irishmen entered the classrooms of the 1950's and 1960's. Whether this means a reawakening of values that once made Ireland famous remains to be seen, as it may just be an American phenomenon; but it at least modified the old peasant's disregard for things intellectual.[12]

American literature in the years since 1923 clearly reflects the absorption of the mass of Irish-Americans into the American landscape. Before World War I, literary figures in the Irish-American community such as John Boyle O'Reilly and Maurice Francis Egan, obviously Irish-Catholics, obviously wrote for Irish-Catholic audiences. They no doubt had talent, but they did not belong to the first class of America's writers. In the years since the Irish have produced a strong list of those who could claim that role, not as Irishmen, but as Americans.

In 1920 both F. Scott Fitzgerald and Eugene O'Neill burst upon the American scene. The former published his first novel, *This Side of Paradise*, while the latter saw his first play performed on Broadway. The lives of both tell much about the Irish experience in America. Fitzgerald's maternal grandfather, Philip McQuillan, came to America in 1843 at the age of nine. Forty-five years later he died and left a small fortune from a wholesale grocery business. His oldest daughter married Edward Fitzgerald. Out of this union came a boy, F. Scott, in 1896. When her husband could not provide a living, she took her family to her mother's home in Saint Paul, Minnesota. In a woman-dominated atmosphere, the young boy grew to manhood with little respect for his father. Although financially secure, the knowledge that he was a descendant of poor peasant Ireland created an embarrassment that his association with wealthy friends only intensified. Like many halfway-up immigrants, he wanted to go all the way and join Protestant America. Enrollment at Newman, a private Catholic college preparatory school outside of Princeton, instead of the more respected and better-known schools of his Protestant friends, further frustrated him. There and later at Princeton he grew to deny his ancestry and his church. He did marry Zelda in a Catholic ceremony, and he did permit the baptism óf his only daughter, but then his relationship with the church ceased. His rapid rise to fame and the resulting publicity completely masked his Irish background. To his readers, he was an American. Only later did the critics discover his Irish ancestry. In the classic sense Fitzgerald lived that old and sad tale in which the unhero, by denying his roots, seeks new ones in a world where, for him, none existed.

O'Neill came from much the same background, but he denied only half of his heritage. His father, born during the Great Famine, emigrated to America and lived in poverty with his large family until he gained financial security through a successful stage career. He married a young Irish girl and soon had three sons, the last Eugene Gladstone. Trained in Catholic schools, the young boy soon lost interest in his religion, but he did not deny his Irish background. By the time he matured, the old stage Irish type had disappeared, but George M. Cohan kept the image of the comic Irishman alive. The typical happy Irishman, Cohan captured the heart of America with his stage portrayals, his songs (he wrote "Over There") and his show, *The Song and Dance Man*. His view of life pleased millions, but it repelled O'Neill, who despised the stage Irish tradition. He, like playwrights of the Abbey Theatre, wanted to tell the real story of the Irish. After his first Broadway play, he dominated American drama with a wide variety of human portraits for a quarter of a century. Forever proud of his background, he often painted pictures of Irish life that did not win the applause of the Irish, but he wrote for a wider audience.

Another literary figure who followed O'Neill and Fitzgerald came from the other side of the tracks. Born in Chicago in 1904, James T. Farrell had a rough-and-ready father. Although he tried, he simply could not support his family. Relatives who held slightly more prestigious positions as clerk, raised the boy in South Side Chicago. There Farrell found the materials for his classic stories of Studs Lonigan and Danny O'Neill. These gave him a place in the first rank of America's writers, and like Eugene O'Neill, he gained prominence by writing the story of the American Irish for all Americans. Also like O'Neill, he forsook his church but not his Irish heritage. [13]

If these men achieved front rank, their fellow Irishmen of second and third generation found numerous doors opening in the world of big business. Matthew McCloskey and John McShain, two Irishmen from Philadelphia, began to build their respective construction empires in the 1930's and 1940's. More Irishmen began to appear in banking and financial circles, the most famous being Joseph P. Kennedy who made millions in real estate, the stock market, and most symbolically the scotch market. [14] By the 1960's they appeared at the head of many of America's most important corporations. Yet again, as in the past, the Irish made their greatest advances in the world of politics, but here a clear difference separated the pre-World War I Irish politician from those who gained power in the postwar era.

II   *Changing Political Scene*

In the nineteenth and early twentieth centuries the Irish climb in politics rested upon Irish voters and ultimately upon their personal association with the Anglo-Irish struggle. In those years an Irishman could win local political offices with relative ease, but he could not move beyond that level unless national issues and voting patterns placed undue significance upon his particular region. This happened in the immediate aftermath of the Civil War, during the 1880's, and less so in Wilson's second administration.

By the turn of the century, this limit upon the rise of Irish politicians started to change. Where Patrick Collins could control a congressional district in only one part of Boston in the 1880's, he won the citywide mayoralty election in 1902. Twelve years later, David I. Walsh became governor of Massachusetts and moved to the United States Senate in 1918. There he met other Irishmen who had earned the right to represent their states, including such influential personalities as James Phelan from California and Thomas I. Walsh from Montana. In the course of World War I the Protestant Irishman, "Wild Bill" Donovan, won national fame as the commander of the mostly Irish-Catholic New York Fighting Sixty-ninth, while the work of young Patrick Hurley in France effectively gained him some important friends, including John J. Pershing and Herbert Hoover. Both Donovan and Hurley would later win important offices in the administrations of Republican Hoover and Democrat Roosevelt. Joe Tumulty, of course, served Woodrow Wilson. In all of these cases the ability to gain statewide elections or to reach high-level posts in the administration rested more upon one's personal abilities and one's relationship to American power than upon his position relative to the Irish-American community. [15]

The career of Al Smith serves as an excellent example of the new world of Irish politicians. For years he had worked his way through the ranks of Tammany Hall like many Irish politicians before him, and he emerged as a candidate for governor of New York in 1918. Victory in that contest started a chain of events that moved the little boy from the Lower East Side and Fulton's Fish Market toward the dream of any politician, a nomination for the presidency of the United States. First nominated in 1920 as a gesture, his honesty, hard work, and shockingly progressive ideas for a Tammany man in Albany, led to a boom for him in 1924. William Gibbs McAdoo and Smith's stand on Prohibition stopped him then, but four years later he ran again and won the Democratic nomination. The urban "Honest Abe," an Irishman with broad-based appeal, had arrived; but he unfortunately ran against rural, conservative, prosperous America and lost. Some claimed his religion sealed his doom, but in reality 1928 was a Republican year. The architect of prosperity, Herbert Hoover, won with ease. This Irish assault on the presidency, made possible by Smith's movement away from the narrow issues that attracted Irish voters, would not be repeated for another thirty-two years, but then the candidate would be an entirely different kind of man.[16]

Smith's loss in 1928 pointed toward a basic shift in American politics. His victories in major cities marked his party as that of urban America, while his relative success with midwestern progressives created a possible alliance between the East and the Midwest. If the party could regain the South, add the eastern cities, and reduce the Republican vote in middle America, its candidate could win. Franklin D. Roosevelt did all that in 1932; and, when he entered the White House, he had to reward the party faithful which included, of course, the Irish. James Farley had managed Roosevelt's campaign for governor of New York in 1928 and for the next four years had led his effort to win the Democratic presidential nomination. In return for his role as campaign manager in 1932, he received the traditional reward, the postmaster-generalship. Roosevelt offered Senator Thomas Walsh of Montana the attorney general's office, and later he offered an important White House staff position to Thomas Corcoran. Frank Murphy accepted the post of governor-general of the Philippines, later returned to Washington as the attorney general, and then received a seat on the Supreme Court. In 1934 Joseph P. Kennedy gained the chairmanship of the newly created Securities Exchange Commission and later went to London as ambassador. Other Irishmen arrived in Congress in this surge toward the Democratic party, but they, like Roosevelt's appointees, gained their positions for reasons unrelated to their Irish origins. Service to the party, a purely American institution, more than anything else, determined their success, and that service meant more than controlling Irish voters in the vanishing "Irish towns" of America's cities. [17]

This pattern of Irish politics did not change with the end of Roosevelt's administration. As World War II closed and Harry Truman assumed the presidency, continued Irish control of the big-city machines gave them a voice in both state and national party circles. J. Howard McGrath of Rhode Island served in the Senate as chairman of the Democratic National Committee and then as Truman's attorney general. The scandals of 1951 forced President Truman to replace McGrath, and he picked James P. McGranery of Philadelphia. Robert Hannegan, an Irish politician from Saint Louis, had befriended Truman in 1940 and engineered his vice-presidential election in 1944. In return, he became Truman's first postmaster general. Maurice Tobin became secretary of labor, and Matthew Connelly worked on the White House staff. [18] For these men, like their predecessors under Roosevelt, their Irish background was only incidental to their success.

At the same time, openings occurred in the Republican party. A number of Irish Republicans won seats in Congress, while William F. Bleakly ran for the governorship of New York in 1936. John Danaher went to the Senate in 1938. Eight years later, Wisconsin sent Joe McCarthy to the Senate. When Dwight D. Eisenhower won the presidency in 1952, he gave the post of secretary of labor to Martin Durkin. When he resigned, the post went to James Mitchell. [19]

If Americans of Irish descent produced a number of respectable leaders in both parties, they also developed a share of the less respectable political types. The Boston Irish, for instance, gave the Democratic party that irascible maverick, James Curley. Born in a Boston slum in 1874, Curley won his first elective office in 1899 and lost his last in 1949. Elected four times to Congress and four times as mayor, he held offices all the way from a member of the city council to governor of Massachusetts. During his incredible career, he lost as many elections as he won. Never part of an organization, Curley relied upon the fears and hopes of his constituents and induced them to believe that only he could fulfill all of their needs. He would do anything to win—fight, lie, cheat—but he led the poor of Boston, which included more than the Irish, against the Boston Yankees and their friends with Harvard degrees. Lacking any sense of commitment except to his own little world, he made little effort to work for anything but to gain power and the joy it gave him to exercise it.[20]

On the Republican side, Joe McCarthy grew up in an "Irish settlement," went to Marquette University, and won his first elective office as a Republican in 1939. From there he forced his way into the Republican senatorial primary in 1946. With false stories filling his campaign literature, he won the nomination and then the election. For three years he remained relatively quiet, until February 9, 1950, when he delivered his first speech on Communists in government at Wheeling, West Virginia. For the next four years, Senator Joe McCarthy led the fight against Communists with a campaign that fed upon the fears and frustrations of millions of Americans.[21] Yet both Curley and McCarthy, while exhibiting much of the Irish character, played distinctly American, not Irish-American, roles. Their lives and style of operation grew out of an American experience to fill an American need.

To a great extent, this style of operation grew naturally out of the economic and social changes that characterized Irish-American life in the fifty years after World War I. Those same changes had profound impact upon Irish control of Tammany Hall. When Charles Murphy died in 1924, Tammany died with him. Poor leadership contributed to Al Smith's failure to gain the Democratic nomination in that year, and, when he ran and lost four years later, the Tammany Irish lost even more prestige. The election of John Currey as boss of Tammany in 1929, his ineffective leadership, and disclosures of widespread corruption with some public scandals included, led to a victory for the Republican, Fiorello La Guardia, in the mayoralty race in 1933. The "braves" of Tammany then removed Currey and elected James J. Dooling to take his place. Continued campaign defeats and Dooling's sudden death in 1937 placed Christopher D. Sullivan in command. This last representative of Tammany's most illustrious family, however, could not restore election prosperity. La Guardia won an unprecedented third term in the mayor's office, and Thomas Dewey uncovered signs of Tammany graft and collusion with criminal elements. In that atmosphere Sullivan lost his post. He was followed by other

Irishmen, but Tammany now had no money. With no power over patronage, they could neither attract members nor pay bills. In 1943 Tammany had to sell its building at Seventeenth Street and Union Square.

A ray of hope came in 1945 when the Irish immigrant, Bill O'Dwyer, won the mayor's office, but a battle with Tammany over patronage erupted early in his term. O'Dwyer had the help of a rising Italian-American politician, Carmine de Sapio, in his attempt to gain control of the "Wigwam," but other problems soon divided the two men. A number of rapid changes in the leadership followed. These ended in July, 1949, when De Sapio gained command of Tammany Hall. In this period of sad decline the Irish continued to rule the Bronx under the competent leadership of Ed Flynn, but he died in 1953, and his power passed to De Sapio. Whether the Irish realized it or not, they had lost control of New York. The Irish population patterns in the city continued to shift in the 1950's, and by the early 1960's everyone realized that New York no longer belonged to the Irish. By then a new Tammany Chief had replaced De Sapio, J. Raymond Jones, the Negro leader of Harlem.

This change in Tammany leadership clearly reflects the kind of watershed the decade of the 1950's became for Americans of Irish descent; but, if it marked a decline in some kinds of political activity, it also marked the start of another attempt to gain the White House. The Irish still controlled some city machines. Mayor Richard Daley ruled Chicago, while William Green stood ready to deliver Philadelphia and David Lawrence could offer Pittsburgh. Charles Buckley of the Bronx offered help in New York, while the leading Democratic Irish family, the Kennedys, already had Boston and the state of Massachusetts, and John Bailey ruled the party in Connecticut. In that atmosphere John Fitzgerald Kennedy made his first move for national prominence in 1956 with a strong showing for the second place on the Democratic ballot, only to lose to Estes Kefauver. For the next four years, Kennedy campaigned for the Democratic nomination with all the forces he could gather and man could buy. When the delegates met in Los Angeles, he had already won the battle. He quickly selected Lyndon Baines Johnson for the second slot. In some areas the religious issue played a significant part, but in spite of it, an American of Irish descent became president of the United States.

The man who delivered his inaugural address on January 20,

1961, however, was not an Irish-American. His ancestors may have traveled to America, and he may have exhibited many of the historical traits of the Irish, but he had no direct relationship with the Irish poor or those recently arrived first-generation Irish who were rapidly finding their homes in American suburbs. He came from an aristocratic family of immense wealth with roots deep in America's political life and received his education at the Boston Latin Grammar school, Choate, and Harvard—scarcely the educational path of Boston Irishmen. His career in the House and Senate created few parallels to what one would expect of an Irish-American with the tendency to remain somewhat independent and sparingly liberal. The campaign itself split the Irish vote, if it existed, and his success was more dependent upon bloc voting of Negroes than of any other group. Yet Kennedy's election did show that America was an open society, that all had a chance, and that "Wasp" America had passed into the realm of history. [22]

In those short three years of his administration, Kennedy tried to build a future power base on the strength of the poor. Impressed with the growing power and awareness of the Negro, he made his appeal in that direction, as much from practical politics as from philosophical commitment, but in the years since Kennedy's endorsement of the liberal dream, the American Irish moved further away from that dream. Negro demands and their success in gaining them have caused serious discussion among all levels of Irishmen in America. The movement from the city and the turnover of their homes to black Americans have accelerated steadily in the past five years, and one hears increasingly at Irish affairs (attended only by the old and a few curious young) that the "black is getting everything, while we pay the taxes." If anything, those who trace their ancestry to Ireland have moved to the political right in the course of the 1960's. [23]

At the start of the 1970's, it appears that the Negro's role in American life may very possibly force the re-emergence of the Irish as a clearly defined pressure group with well-established aims and the means necessary to gain them. The Negro's success in the 1960's has already caused other white ethnic groups to reconsider their roles in American society, to seek government aid to fulfill those roles and to prepare specific goals for the coming decade. Using the same tactics of the successful Negro drive of the 1960's, they will demand the same favors. In fact, government has already recognized their needs. Congress passed an Ethnic Studies bill that will finance the understanding of ethnicity in American life. Yet there is no guarantee that the American Irish will follow the example of other ethnic groups. Even though they complain about the Negro, they speak not as ethnics, but as Americans who live in certain areas, who believe in certain values and who wish to see them implemented.[24]

If the American scene will not awaken the old force, the crisis of the Irish Catholics in Belfast might. What began as an authentic civil rights movement on the part of Catholics against the Protestant majority in Northern Ireland in 1968 quickly became a battle for the end of the partition of Ireland. The civil rights phase captured the imagination of many Americans and organizations to aid the Catholics in Ulster quickly appeared in America. Using the old techniques, they collected funds and sponsored tours of such leaders of the Northern Irish movement as Bernadette Devlin. Some have claimed that large sums were collected in this way, but this is not strictly true. The Devlin tour ended in failure as large numbers of American-Irish ignored her. She made a number of tactical blunders, including her references to the Negro struggle in America as synonymous with the Catholic struggle in Ireland. The vast majority of the American Irish simply did not care. In their middle-class homes in white suburbia they enjoy the good life America offers and this they do not want disturbed. The Ulster struggle then fell into the hands of the IRA and daily terrorist attacks occurred throughout Northern Ireland in 1970. The British responded with the shipment of troops to preserve the peace and by 1970 authorities in Ulster answered the continued terrorist attacks with an internment policy which permitted arrest without trial and on mere suspicion. Whatever the name, it smacked of an old British solution to Irish troubles, one used on numerous occasions in the years after 1691. As a result, support for the IRA both in Ireland and America grew quickly; but, unfortunately, the IRA divided over the use of violence. One wing recommended widespread violence, while the moderates felt that excessive force would only hurt their chances of ultimate success. This division not only weakened the resistance in Northern Ireland, but it caused divisions among IRA sympathizers in Ireland and among the Irish in America. Extreme violence won little support among the majority of the Irish in America in spite of claims to the contrary. The older generations simply did not, and will not, contribute to that kind of thing and even those immigrants who arrived in the last twenty years tend to avoid it. Only those who have come from Ulster in recent years, who have families in the distressed areas, and who remember the misery of their early life, have any real commitment to this kind of campaign.

Meanwhile, as the terrorist campaign captured the headlines of the world press, the British Army settled down to a policy of keeping the Protestants and Catholics apart, while other authorities searched for more permanent solutions. In such an atmosphere of high tension another crisis came in February, 1972 when British troops fired into a crowd of Catholic demonstrators, killing thirteen people. The latest "Bloody Sunday" in the history of the unhappy country quickly caused Irish sentiments around the world to rise and money to flow to Ireland from America, mainly through the Northern Irish Aid Committee. Yet even this incident did not permanently change the pattern of support among the American Irish. The claim that huge sums have been collected appears unwarranted. In Philadelphia, for instance, the Irish have contributed no more than $100,000 in the four years of the crisis. Although the Irish in other cities such as New York, Boston, and Chicago have sent more, in comparison to the vast sums sent in the 1880's and during World War I today's totals remain small.[25]

If conditions in Ireland deteriorate further, this lack of commitment on the part of the American Irish may change into genuine involvement, but that appears unlikely. The suspension of the Belfast government and direct rule by England created an atmosphere for political maneuvering that the Northern Irish government did not possess. In addition the reaction to the constant terrorism spreads daily and demands to end it now come from all sides. This caused both wings of the IRA to accept an uneasy truce by the summer of 1972 and by the Fall the wild leadership of the extremist wing fell from power. As 1972 closed, that particular phase of the struggle appears to have run its course.

If a temporary solution is not found, matters in Ireland get worse, and the American Irish do become involved, they could not resort to methods they used in the past. Although they can on occasion force a particular American politician to issue a statement, they can not force American intervention in Anglo-Irish affairs as they did in the 1880's and during World War I. The Irish simply no longer possess the power they once did in America's politics. If the events of the Democratic Convention in July, 1972 offer any signs of the future, the power of the Irish in that party has waned. Richard Daley's failure to appear in Miami marked, not just a victory for the new, but the death of the old leadership.

The memories of what it was to be Irish in America have undoubtedly faded. All that remains of the force, once powerful enough to threaten the enormous English Empire of the nineteenth century, is the claim to Irish descent. The American Irish stopped being Irish-Americans some fifty years ago and today they are more American than Irish and they want to stay that way. Although some may deny it, the Irish have disappeared as a political force in America. Some claim that this is because they are no longer hungry, that they have over-acculturated, that they are the victims of their mothers,[26] that they are more "Wasp" than "Wasps", but the real reason is that they no longer have a reason to act as a pressure group.

Epilogue

I RELAND's geography clearly created a people with an interest in independence and a tendency to ignore the outside world. Her history only intensified those characteristics. Neither Saint Patrick's introduction of Christianity nor the numerous English attempts to control the island during the Middle Ages destroyed that parochialism. The introduction of Protestantism to England in the sixteenth century meant that religion would help to keep the Irish spirit for independence alive. When Elizabeth, James I, and Cromwell attempted to pacify the island through the process of plantations, they added the economic factor to Anglo-Irish relations. In the following century, the Penal Codes literally created a whole class of people whose hatred of all things English defied description. English failure to solve the questions of population, land, and food in the first half of the nineteenth century led to the Great Famine, which created in the heart of the peasant class who came to America a bitter hatred of England. The Irish Question, which continued into the twentieth century, thus had deep political, economic, social and religious roots, all of which the ex-peasants carried with them as they crossed the Atlantic.

The America these immigrants found in the late 1840's was in the process of finding how to live in the aftermath of the hectic days of Jacksonian democracy. From the vantage point of mid-twentieth-century America, it appears clear that America had, from the start, grown in the atmosphere of a pluralistic world. This was especially true in the eighteenth century when the influx of numerous immigrants intensified the faction politics practiced in the colonial assemblies. The nationalization of such politics during the Revolutionary War, however, did not lead directly to party politics, and only after the signing of the Constitution did the difference between Hamiltonian and Jeffersonian thinking contribute the concept of the political party to American political life. Yet, neither Hamilton nor Jefferson created parties with durability. Only after Jackson appeared on the scene did Americans find a party that would last and only because Jackson's appearance marked the emergence of the modern political boss. Americans had not quite digested that fact when the Irish arrived in large numbers in the late 1840's and early 1850's. They came at the right moment to participate in the perfection of the new politics as an expression of American pluralism.

At the same time the conditions in Ireland in the late 1840's combined to create the elements necessary for a pressure group to gain success in America. The misery of the famine drove hundreds of thousands to America, and the abortive revolution of the Young Irelanders provided men who could lead these masses. The reception received in America only intensified their hatred of England. Thus were created the masses, the leaders, and the issue that would unite. By the end of the 1850's, just as America was stumbling into civil war, the Irish in America became aware of their potential power.

The Civil War offered the Irish enormous opportunities to gain a sense of belonging in their new land. It also created a situation in which they organized an authentic national body. At the end of the war, political and diplomatic events permitted the Irish to employ their power in support of Ireland's claim for independence. As that unique cluster of events developed, they pressured Congress and the White House and won significant concessions from both. Grant's election, the successful negotiations that led to the Treaty of Washington, and Gladstone's first administration in England, however, ended this atmosphere. Irish power in America collapsed, and for the next decade, the Irish-American concentrated upon his own problems and, in spite of setbacks, grew in respectability and slowly improved his economic lot.

The question of Ireland, however, remained, and as the 1870's drew to a close, the unique situation of the immediate post-Civil War years reappeared. The close balance of political power that existed in America from 1876 to 1896 forced politicians to seek issues that would cause little loss of political power, yet gain enough votes to win. In that context, both major political parties rediscovered the old American animosity toward England. A political intensification of Anglophobia created problems for

English and American diplomats, which England tried to ignore, but America's politicians accepted the cost because they believed they could capture a significant segment of voters—the Irish—without alienating their normal supporters. At that precise moment when the Irish gained the ability to influence national politics, Parnell unified the Irish behind an assault on the Irish land question and a demand for Home Rule. The Irish in America followed his lead, and for a decade that chance cluster of events permitted the Irish-Americans to operate as a successful pressure group.

Their own blunders, the death of Parnell, the emergence of the Republicans as the majority party in the late 1890's, and growing rapprochement between England and America seriously reduced Irish power at the national level in the twenty years from 1890 to 1910. Once again, the focus of their activity shifted to the problem of making a secure place for themselves in American society. By the start of the twentieth century, they could look back upon a long upward climb. The distinctions between those who had made it and those who had not became clear. Though they had made their contributions felt in various fields, their dominance was mainly in the church and in local politics. Devotion to the Democrats did give them claims on that party for favors and gradually some Irish bosses began to think of wider political possibilities. But they made no serious attempt to achieve them until after 1910.

Behind all of these accomplishments, however, loomed the question of Ireland's freedom and by 1910 conditions again moved in the direction that would permit the Irish to use their power in America to fight for this objective. A revitalized radical wing of Irish-American nationalism reappeared just as the dream of independence rekindled in Ireland. At the same time, the Progressive movement in America created new political divisions and increased the possibilities that a swing vote could gain enormous power, yet these did not develop sufficiently to permit the American Irish any real influence in the 1912 elections, and before they could develop sufficiently to re-create the atmosphere of the 1880's, World War I erupted.

The new situation quickly forced events both in Ireland and in America into the hands of the radicals. Devoy felt he could best help Ireland by working for a German victory over England. Yet that effort failed in Easter Week of 1916.

Wilson then won reelection in spite of some Irish opposition in the following autumn, and in the spring of 1917 America declared war on Germany. For nine months Irish-Americans saw little hope that Ireland would gain her freedom as a result of the war, but Wilson's pronouncement on self-determination provided the spark to organize again for a final effort on behalf of Ireland. For the next eighteen months, they fought for Wilson's ear, but the president failed to fulfill the expectations he had created. The bitterness of defeat caused the full force of Irish opinion to attack Wilson's treaty and the League of Nations. After the Irish contributed to the defeat of both the Republicans returned to office, England settled the Irish Question in 1923, and the Irish in America faded into the mass that was America.

In the 1930's and 1940's, Irishmen were absorbed into American life, pursuing their careers as Americans and not as Irish-Americans. By the 1950's, they had formed strong loyalties to their various economic groups, their American neighborhoods, and their professions. They viewed the world from the perspective of their new loyalties and voted in accordance with them. In the years after 1923 their attachment to Ireland died. Ireland no longer needed them nor they her.

Though Irish-American contributions to the United States, as these pages indicate, are many and varied, their role in politics stands out. They were the first to perfect the political methods made possible by Jacksonian democracy. They were able to achieve it because they possessed the basic characteristics—adequate leadership, large numbers, and an issue to unite both—that made a pressure group politically successful in America. Not until the twentieth century were they seriously challenged in their political power, but the residue of their earlier work kept them in command for another half century. Only in the 1950's did they start to give way, and only in the 1960's did others come to dominate where the Irish had ruled supreme for so many years.

No one can foretell the future. The Irish may once again emerge as a political force in American life, or they may elect to remain as only elements in various interest groups. In either case, one can expect to find them cherishing the characteristics that made their story possible—pride in an enviable past, unquenchable thirst for independence, great wit, relaxing charm, and a drive to accomplish that rests upon a firm belief in God and in the afterworld that is His.

Notes

1. J. H. Andrews, "A Geographer's View of Irish History," in *The Course of Irish History*, T. W. Moody and F. X. Martin, eds. (New York: Weybright and Talley, 1967), 17–29. This book, based upon a series of radio lectures, has a number of excellent chapters. The best study is still Edmund Curtis, *The History of Ireland*, 6th ed. (London: Methuen, 1965).

2. A. J. Otway-Ruthven, *A History of Medieval Ireland* (London: Ernest Benn, 1968), 1–14.

3. Giovanni Costigan, *A History of Modern Ireland* (New York: Pegasus, 1970), 19–29. See also Maire and Liam de Paor, *Early Christian Ireland*, 2nd ed. (London: Thomas and Hudson, 1960), 1–130.

4. Liam de Paor, "The Age of the Viking Wars," in *The Course of Irish History*, 91–106; Liam de Paor, *Early Christian Ireland*, 131–60; Otway-Ruthven, *Medieval Ireland*, 24–33.

5. Edmund Curtis, *History of Medieval Ireland from 1086 to 1513*, 2nd ed. (London: Methuen, 1938), Chapters 1 and 2.

6. Rev. F. S. Martin, "The Anglo-Norman Invasion," in *The Course of Irish History*, 123–43, gives a good short explanation of this question. Both Curtis and Otway-Ruthven, in their respective studies of medieval Ireland cited above, go into greater detail.

7. The Irish resurgence is told by J. F. Lyon, "The Medieval English Colony," and by A. Cosgrove, "The Gaelic Resurgence and the Geraldine Supremacy," both of which appear in *The Course of Irish History* as Chapters 9 and 10, respectively. Again, Curtis and Otway-Ruthven are also available for more detailed information.

8. A short but adequate description of Poyning's Law and the story of Silken Thomas can be found in Costigan, *Modern Ireland*, 46–49.

9. J. C. Beckett, *The Making of Modern Ireland, 1603–1923* (London: Faber and Faber, 1966), 13–24.

10. For the detail of the early Stuarts see A. Clarke, "The Colonization of Ulster and the Rebellion of 1641," in *The Course of Irish History*, 187–203; and Beckett, *Modern Ireland*, 40–115.

11. John G. Simms, *Jacobite Ireland, 1685–1691* (London: Routledge and Kegan Paul, 1969), is the latest study of this period.

12. One cannot quite understand Ireland in the eighteenth century without careful reading of J. C. Beckett's *Protestant Dissent in Ireland, 1687–1780* (London: Faber and Faber, 1948) and Maureen Wall's *The Penal Laws, 1687–1780: Church and State from the Treaty of Limerick to the Accession of George III* (Dundale: Dublin Historical Association, 1961). Beckett covers this period well in his broader study *Modern Ireland*, and Wall did the chapter in *The Course of Irish History* that covers these years.

13. The impact of the American Revolution is shown in Maurice R. O'Connell's *Irish Politics and Social Conflict in the Age of the American Revolution* (Philadelphia: University of Pennsylvania Press, 1965). Edith Johnston, *Great Britain and Ireland, 1760–1800: A Study in Political Administration* (Edinburgh: University of St. Andrews, 1963) and R. B. McDowell, *Irish Public Opinion, 1750–1800* (London: Faber and Faber, 1944) also should be read for this period. McDowell wrote the chapter on this period for *The Course of Irish History*.

14. In addition to Johnston's book cited above, one should also read Stephen Gwynn's *Henry Grattan and His Times* (London: Brown and Nolan, 1939) to learn the details of Grattan's party.

15. Rosamund Jacob, *The Rise of the United Irishmen, 1791–94* (London: G. G. Harrap & Co., 1937) tells this story in detail. See also Hereward Senior, *Orangeism in Ireland and Britain, 1795–1836* (New York: Hillary, 1966).

16. O'Connell's career is covered in Sean O'Faolain, *King of the Beggars* (New York: Viking Press, 1938). A different approach is found in Denis Gwynn, *Daniel O'Connell* (Cork: Cork University Press, 1947). This is a revised edition of the 1929 study. See also Lawrence J. McCaffrey, *Daniel O'Connell and the Repeal Year* (Lexington: University of Kentucky Press, 1966) and Angus MacIntyre, *The Liberation: Daniel O'Connell and the Irish Party* (New York: Macmillan, 1965).

17. Thomas N. Brown, *Irish-American Nationalism* (Philadelphia: Lippincott, 1966), argues well that this is precisely what happened.

CHAPTER 2

1. Wallace Notestein, *The English People on the Eve of Colonization* (New York: Harper & Row, 1954), 3. Notestein claims that the English are a composite people but, because the waves of immigration came slowly, the population became thoroughly mixed. I would hold that, during the medieval period, the English failure to mix thoroughly created English political concepts.

2. The story of these developments can be found in great detail in Charles M. Andrews, *The Colonial Period of American History*, 4 vols. (New Haven: Yale University Press, 1934).

3. The story of why the Ulster Scots left Ireland is told in R. J. Dickinson, *Ulster Emigration to Colonial America, 1718–1775* (London: Routledge and Kegan Paul, 1966).

4. For the story of the Scotch-Irish once they arrived in America, see H. J. Ford, *The Scotch-Irish in America* (Princeton: Princeton University Press, 1915) and the more recent study, James G. Leyburn, *The Scotch Irish: A Social History* (Chapel Hill: University of North Carolina Press, 1962).

5. The story of those various groups can be found in numerous books. One short description is found in Maldwyn Allen Jones, *American Immigration* (Chicago: University of Chicago Press, 1960), 16–31. See his bibliography for Chapter 1, 326–28. See also Carl Wittke, *We Who Built America*, rev. ed. (Cleveland: Press of Case Western Reserve University, 1967).

6. For the problem of the power of the Assembly see J. P. Greene, *The Quest for Power: The Lower Houses of Assembly in the Southern Royal Colonies* (Chapel Hill: University of North Carolina Press, 1963). For the more general concepts see J. P. Greene, "Changing Interpretations of Early American Politics," in *The Reinterpretation of Early American History*, ed. by R. A. Billington (San Marino: The Huntington Library, 1966), 151–84.

7. J. Franklin Jamison, *The American Revolution Considered as a Social Movement* (Boston: Beacon Press, 1956), 12–18, and Jones, *American Immigration*, 53–57.

8. For this story of the origins of the political parties, see Joseph Charles, *The Origins of the American Party System* (New York: Harper Torchbook Edition, 1961), and William Nesbitt Chambers, *Political Parties in a New Nation* (New York: Oxford University Press, 1963). A number of studies at the state level clarify these points. For the latest see J. Banner, Jr., *To the Hartford Convention: The Federalists and the Origins of Party Politics in Massachusetts, 1789–1815* (New York: Knopf, 1970).

9. Jones, *American Immigration*, 65–69, 74–75; John Claiborne, *Seventy-Five Years in Old Virginia* (New York: Macmillan, 1904), 28, 117.

10. John C. Miller, *Crisis in Freedom, The Alien and Sedition Acts* (Boston: Little, Brown, 1951), tells the full story.

11. Carl Wittke, *The Irish in America* (Baton Rouge: Louisiana State University Press, 1956), 203.

12. W. F. Adams, *Ireland and Irish Emigration to the New World from 1815 to the Famine* (New Haven: Yale University Press, 1932), 334–409. See Paul J. Foik, "Pioneer Efforts in Catholic Journalism in the United States, 1809–1840," *The Catholic Historical Review*, I (1916), 258–70, and Thomas J. Moriarty, "The Truth Teller and Irish Americana of the 1820's" *Records* of the American Catholic Historical Society of Philadelphia, LXXV (March, 1964), 39–52.

13. The best summary of the period is still George Dangerfield, *The Era of Good Feelings* (New York: Harcourt, Brace & World, 1952).

14. The literature on Jackson and his period is extensive, but the best survey is Glyndon G. Van Deusen, *The Jacksonian Era, 1828–1848* (New York: Harper & Row, 1964).

15. See Chapter 8 in Lee Benson, *The Concept of Jacksonian Democracy: New York as a Test Case* (New York: Atheneum, 1964); Wittke, *The Irish in America*, 106–7; M. R. Weiner, *Tammany Hall* (New York: Doubleday, Doran, 1928), 26–31.

CHAPTER 3

1. Nicholas Mansergh, *The Irish Question, 1840–1921* (London: George Unwin, 1965), 19–55. See also Conrad Arensberg and Solon T. Kimball, *Family and Community in Ireland* (Cambridge: Harvard University Press, 1968).

2. J. C. Beckett, *The Making of Modern Ireland*, 150–186; Maureen Wall, "The Age of the Penal Laws," in *The Course of Irish History*, 217–31.

3. John E. Pomfret, *The Struggle for Land in Ireland, 1800–1923* (Princeton: Princeton University Press, 1930), 1–33.

4. Cecil Woodham-Smith, *The Great Hunger* (New York: Harper & Row, 1962), Chapter I.

5. R. D. Edwards and T. D. Williams, eds., *The Great Famine: Studies in Irish History, 1845–52* (New York: New York University Press, 1957) should also be read for the study of the Famine.

6. Beckett, *The Making of Modern Ireland*, 332–335; Kevin D. Nowlan, "The Political Background," in *The Great Famine*, 187–203.

7. For the effect of the Famine, see E. R. R. Green, "The Great Famine," in *The Course of Irish History*, 273–274, and Beckett, *The Making of Modern Ireland*, 348–50. The story of the movement to America is found in numerous places. See Francis Morehouse, "The Irish Migration of the Forties," *American Historical Review*, XXXIII (1927–28), 579–92.

8. Nowlan, "The Political Background," 206; Oliver MacDonagh, "Irish Emigration to the United States of America and the British Colonies During the Famine," in *The Great Famine*, 377–87.

9. Brown, *Irish-American Nationalism*, 17–41.

10. Adams, *Ireland and Irish Migration*, 371–84; Wittke, *The Irish in America*, 109.

11. John Higham, *Strangers in the Land: Patterns of American Nativism, 1860–1925* (New York: Atheneum, 1965), 3–11.

12. Brown, *Irish-American Nationalism*, 23; Phillip H. Bagenal, *The American Irish* (Boston: Roberts Brothers, 1882), 110.

13. Brian Jenkins, *Fenians and Anglo-American Relations During Reconstruction* (Ithaca and London: Cornell University Press, 1969), 12–23;

William D'Arcy, *The Fenian Movement in the United States, 1858–1886* (Washington: The Catholic University of America Press, 1947), tells the full story.

14. Beckett, *The Making of Modern Ireland*, 358–59; D'Arcy, *The Fenian Movement*, 12.

CHAPTER 4

1. The literature on the coming of the Civil War is, of course, enormous, but I owe my own understanding of these events to a former teacher, Roy F. Nichols, *The Disruption of American Democracy* (New York: Macmillan, 1948).

2. Wittke, *The Irish in America*, 125–130.

3. *The Eighth Census, 1860: The Statistics of the Population of the United States*, 4 vols. (Washington: Government Printing Office, 1864–66), I, xxii, xxix, xxx. Carl Wittke, *We Who Built America* (Cleveland: The Press of Western Reserve University, 1964).

4. Emerson D. Fite, *The Presidential Campaign of 1860* (Port Washington, N.Y.: Kennikut Press, 1967). This is a reprint of a 1911 study that gives all of the details.

5. Florence S. Gibson, *The Attitudes of the New York Irish Toward State and National Affairs, 1848–92*, (New York: Columbia University Press, 1951), 111–40; Joseph P. O'Grady, "Anthony M. Keiley (1832–1905): Virginia's Catholic Politician," *The Catholic Historical Review*, LIV, (January, 1969), 621.

6. See Ella Lonn's books, *Foreigners in the Union Army and Navy* (Baton Rouge: Louisiana State University Press, 1951), and *Foreigners in the Confederacy* (Chapel Hill: University of North Carolina Press, 1940), for these details.

7. Gibson, *Attitudes of the New York Irish*, 142–58; J. McCague, *The Second Rebellion* (New York: The Dial Press, 1968).

8. Thomas A. Bailey, *A Diplomatic History of the American People*, 8th ed. (New York: Appleton-Century-Crofts, 1969), 319.

9. The two classic studies are still E. D. Adams, *Great Britain and the American Civil War*, 2 vols. (London: Russell and Russell, 1925), and Q. L. Owsley, *King Cotton Diplomacy*, 2nd ed. rev. (Chicago: University of Chicago Press, 1959).

10. Beckett, *The Making of Modern Ireland*, 353–58; *A History of Modern Ireland*, 207–8.

11. D'Arcy, *The Fenian Movement*, 12–37.

12. *Ibid.*, 80–81.

13. La Wanda Cox and John H. Cox, *Politics, Principles and Prejudice, 1865–66: Dilemma of Reconstruction America* (New York: Macmillan, 1963), tells the story in great detail.

14. Jenkins, *Fenian and Anglo-American Relations*, 248–81.

15. D'Arcy, *The Fenian Movement*, 64, 65, 186; John A. Cuddy, "The Influence of the Fenian Movement on Anglo-American Relations, 1860–1872," unpublished doctoral dissertation, (Saint John's University, 1953), 19, 108; Major Henri Le Caron, *Twenty-five Years in the Secret Service* (London: Heinemann, 1892), 31, 58.

16. Beckett, *The History of Modern Ireland*, 361.

17. Allan Nevins, *Hamilton Fish: The Inner History of the Grant Administration* (New York: Dodd, Mead, 1936) gives the details here.

18. Arthur H. De Rosier, "Investigation in Failure: The Fenian Raids of 1866–1871," *Southern Quarterly*, III (1965), 181–97.

CHAPTER 5

1. Wittke, *The Irish in America*, 62, 63, 195, 196, 199; Petersburg, *Daily Democrat*, March 1, 20, 1855.

2. For the story of the Irish on the frontier see James P. Shannon, *Catholic Colonization on the Western Frontier* (New Haven: Yale University Press, 1957), and Sister Mary Gilbert Kelly, *Catholic Immigrant Projects in the United States: 1815–1860* (New York: United States Catholic Historical Society, 1939).

3. Sister Joan Marie Donohue, *The Irish Catholic Benevolent Union* (Washington: The Catholic University of America Press, 1953), tells the whole story, while Sister Joan Bland, *The Hibernian Crusade* (Washington: The Catholic University of America Press, 1951), gives another example of a rising national movement. For the AOH see John O'Dea, *History of the Ancient Order of Hibernians and Ladies Auxiliary* 4 vols. (Philadelphia: The Ancient Order of Hibernians, 1923).

4. Wittke, *The Irish in America*, 52–61.

5. *Ibid.*, 216–27.

6. W. G. Broehl, *The Molly Maguires* (Cambridge: Harvard University Press, 1964), gives the scholarly version, while A. H. Lewis, *Lament for the Molly Maguires* (New York: Harcourt Brace, 1964), gives a popular viewpoint.

7. Richard Knowles Morris, *John P. Holland: 1841–1914, Inventor of the Modern Submarine* (Annapolis: The United States Naval Institute, 1966), tells the full story.

8. The lives of many such men can be found in the *Journal of the American Irish Historical Society*.

9. Harold G. Syrett, *The City of Brooklyn: 1867–1898* (New York: Columbia University Press, 1944), 71; Gibson, *The Attitudes of the New York Irish*, 393; Henri Le Caron, *Twenty-Five Years*, 63, 74; O'Brien, *Post Bag*, 11, 563; *Bibliographical Directory of Congress*, 1143, 1745.

10. M. P. Curran, *The Life of Patrick A. Collins* (Norwood, 1903).

11. For Tammany Hall see M. R. Weiner, *Tammany Hall* (New York: Doubleday, Doran, 1928); Alfred Connable and Edward Silberfarb, *Tigers of Tammany* (New York: Doubleday, Doran, 1968).

12. *American*, I (1880), 42.

CHAPTER 6

1. Conor C. O'Brien, *Parnell and His Party: 1880–1890* (Oxford: Clarendon Press, 1957), 161. Sir William Harcourt, the home secretary in William Gladstone's second government, has accurately perceived: "In former rebellions, the Irish were in Ireland. We could reach their forces, cut off their reserves in men and money and then to subjugate them was comparatively easy. Now, there is an Irish nation in the United States, equally hostile, with plenty of money, absolutely beyond our reach and yet within ten days' sail of our shores."

2. Thomas N. Brown, "The Origins and Character of Irish-American Nationalism," *Review of Politics*, XVIII (1956), 345. This is an earlier version of Brown's views that grew out of his dissertation at Harvard.

3. James J. Roche, *The Life of John Boyle O'Reilly* (New York: The Mershon Co., 1891), 143; Le Caron, *Twenty-Five Years*, 107, 109; Brown, *Irish-American Nationalism*.

4. David Thornley, *Issac Butt and Home Rule* (London: Maggilihan and Kee, 1964), carries the story down to 1879 and Butt's death.

5. Norman D. Palmer, *The Irish Land League Crisis* (New Haven: Yale University Press, 1940), 2; Handlin, *Boston's Immigrants*, 34–43.

6. O'Brien, *Parnell and His Party*, 1; Michael Davitt, *The Fall of Feudalism in Ireland* (New York: Harper and Brothers, 1904), 116, 137; Brown, *Irish-American Nationalism*, 85–98. He argues against Davitt's version of all this, but it is clear that he played a mighty role. See T. W. Moody, "Irish-American Nationalism," *Irish Historical Studies*, XV (September, 1967), 438–45, for a discussion of Brown's book.

7. W. Dean Burnham, *Presidential Ballots: 1836–1892* (Baltimore: Johns Hopkins Press, 1955), 34, 118, 130; *American*, V (1882), 65; H. C. Thomas, *The Return of the Democratic Party to Power in 1884* (New York: Columbia University Press, 1919), 15, 228; Harry J. Siever, *Benjamin Harrison: Hoosier Statesman*, 2 vols. (New York: University Publishers, 1959), I, 300.

8. Herbert J. Clancy, *The Presidential Election of 1880* (Chicago: Loyola University Press, 1958), 162; Thomas, *The Return in 1884*, 15; James Bryce, *The American Commonwealth*, 2 vols. (New York: Macmillan, 1889), I, 653, 657, 658.

9. *American*, VII (1883), 310; Gail Hamilton, *Biography of James G. Blaine* (Norwich, Connecticut: The Henry Bill Publishing Co., 1895), 577; Walker Blaine, "Why Harrison Was Elected," *North American Review*.

10. Joseph P. O'Grady, "Irish-Americans and Anglo-American Relations, 1880–1888," unpublished doctoral dissertation (University of Pennsylvania, 1965), Chapter 3.

11. Henrietta M. A. Ward, *Memoirs of Ninety Years*, 2nd ed. (New York: Henry Holt, 1925), 207.

12. Kenneth E. Colton, "Parnell's Mission to Iowa," *Annals of Iowa*, XXII (1940), 312; Michael Davitt, *The Fall of Feudalism in Ireland* (New York: Harper and Brothers, 1904), 194–245.

13. Conor Cruise O'Brien, *Parnell and His Party*, 36.

14. William R. Grace, *The Irish in America* (Chicago: McDonnell Brothers, 1886), 19; Edward A. Jameson, "Irish-Americans, The Irish Question and American Diplomacy; 1895–1921," unpublished doctoral dissertation (Harvard University, 1944), 2 vols. I, 3, 5.

15. O'Grady, "Irish-Americans and Anglo-American Relations, 1880–1888," 36, 38.

16. *Ibid.*, 39–43.

17. O'Brien, *Parnell and His Party*, 49–50; J. L. Hammon, *Gladstone and the Irish Nation* (London: Longmans, Green, 1938), 192.

18. Davitt, *Fall of Feudalism*, 188, 257; William O'Brien and Desmond Ryan, eds., *Devoy's Post Bag, 1871–1928*, 2 vols. (Dublin: Fallon, 1948–1953), 533.

19. Davitt, *Fall of Feudalism*, 257, 308, 365; Hammond, *Gladstone*, 214–215; O'Brien, *Parnell and His Party*, 60; Palmer, *Land League Crisis*, 284.

20. Brown, *Irish-American Nationalism*; O'Grady, "Irish-Americans and Anglo-American Relations," 82–85.

21. L. P. Curtis, Jr., *Coercion and Conciliation in Ireland, 1882–1892: A Study in Conservative Unionism* (Princeton: Princeton University Press, 1963), 15, 33.

CHAPTER 7

1. O'Grady, "Irish-Americans and Anglo-American Relations," 168–178.

2. West to Granville, November 14, 1882, in Paul Knaplund and C. M. Clewes, eds., "Private Letters from the British Embassy in Washington to the Foreign Secretary, Lord Granville, 1880–1885," *American Historical Association Annual Report*, 1941 (Washington: Government Printing Office, 1942), 172; Gibson, *The New York Irish*, 374.

3. O'Grady, "Irish-Americans and Anglo-American Relations," 180–98; Pletcher, *The Awkward Years*, 257–69.

4. Brown, *Irish-American Nationalism*; Curran, *Patrick A. Collins*, 591; Donohue, *Irish Catholic Benevolent Union*, 16, 22; O'Grady, "Anthony M. Keiley," 634–35.

5. O'Grady, "Irish-American and Anglo-American Relations," 199–202.

6. O'Brien, *Parnell and His Party*, 89–98, 165; Joseph Chamberlain, *A Political Memoir: 1880–1892* (London: Batchworth Press, 1953), 88, 161, 168.

7. O'Brien, *Parnell and His Party*, 195; Le Caron, *Twenty-Five Years*, 247; William O'Brien, *Evening Memories* (Dublin: Maunsell & Co., 1920) 136–39.

8. *Public Opinion* II (1886) 63, 409, 467, 506.

9. O'Grady, "Irish-Americans and Anglo-American Relations," 203–83.

10. "Power of the Irish in American Cities," *Living Age*, CLXXXI (November, 1886), 382–84.

11. Pomfret, *Struggle for the Land*, 242; O'Brien, *Parnell and His Party*, 201–15.

12. O'Grady, "Irish-Americans and Anglo-American Relations," 61–68.

13. Blaine to Harrison, May 22, 1889; Blaine to Harrison, September 16, 1891, in A. T. Volweiler, ed., *The Correspondence Between Benjamin Harrison and James G. Blaine: 1888–1893* (Philadelphia: American Philosophical Society, 1940), 64, 186.

14. Francis Lyons, *The Fall of Parnell, 1890–91* (London: Routledge and Kegan Paul, 1960); Curtis, *Coercion and Conciliation*, 301–30; Jules Abels, *The Parnell Tragedy* (London: Bodley, Head, 1966).

15. Henry Hunt, *The Crime of the Century* (Chicago: People's Publishing Co., 1889).

16. George H. Knoles, *The Presidential Campaign and Election of 1892* (Stanford: Stanford University Press, 1942), and Stanley L. Jones, *The Presidential Election of 1896* (Madison: University of Wisconsin Press, 1964), give the details on these campaigns.

CHAPTER 8

1. Edward A. Jamison, "Irish-Americans, The Irish Question and American Diplomacy, 1895–1921," unpublished doctoral dissertation (Harvard University, 1944), covers these years, but he must be used with great caution. For another view, see Alan J. Ward, *Ireland and Anglo-American Relations, 1899–1921* (London: London School of Economics, 1969).

2. Burnham, *Presidential Ballots*, 130; Arthur Link, *The American Epoch* (New York: Knopf, 1969).

3. Bradford Perkins, *The Great Rapprochement: England and the United States, 1895–1914* (New York: Atheneum, 1968). See also Frank T. Reuter, *Catholic Influence on American Colonial Policies, 1898–1904* (Austin: University of Texas Press, 1967).

4. Robert J. Creighton, "Influence of Foreign Issues on American Politics," *International Review*, XIII (1882), 185; Bagenal, *The American*

Irish, 60; anonymous, "Power of the Irish in American Cities," *Living Age,* CLXXI (November, 1886), 382–84; John P. Bobcok, "The Irish Conquest of Our Cities," *Forum,* XVII (1894), 186–95.

5. Curran, *The Life of Patrick A. Collins.*

6. For Croker's life see Alfred H. Lewis, *Richard Croker* (New York: Life Publishing Co., 1901), and Theodore Lothrop Stoddard, *Master of Manhattan: The Life of Richard Croker* (New York: Longmans Green, 1931). There is no biography of Murphy. For a short study, see Connable and Silberfarb, *Tigers of Tammany,* Chapter 8.

7. John J. Meng, "Cahensylism: The First Stage, 1883–1891," *Catholic Historical Review,* XXXI (1946), 389–413, XXXII (1946), 302–40, 389–413; Colman J. Barry, *The Catholic Church and German-Americans;* Thomas T. McAvoy, *The Great Crisis in American Catholic History, 1895–1900* (Chicago: Henry Regency, 1958). For the general story of the Church see T. T. McAvoy, *A History of the Catholic Church in the United States* (South Bend: University of Notre Dame Press, 1969).

8. Higham, *Strangers in the Land,* 79–86, 108.

9. Wittke, *We Who Built America,* 137, 161–2, 475–76.

10. Donahue, *The Irish-Catholic Benevolent Union,* 201 ff.

11. Wittke, *The Irish in America,* 271, Dickson, *Ulster Emigration to Colonial America,* 296–97, for a comment on O'Brien's work.

12. Brown, *Irish-American Nationalism,* 45–46.

13. Edd Winfield Parks, *Southern Poets: Representatives Selections with Introduction, Bibliography and Notes* (New York: American Book Company, 1936), cxi–cxii, cxviii–cxix, 162–68.

14. Maurice Francis Egan, *Recollection of a Happy Life* (New York: Gary H. Doran Company, 1924), 144, 371, 374.

15. William V. Shannon, *The American Irish.* (New York: Macmillan, 1963), 95–102.

16. Wittke, *The Irish in America,* 264–72.

17. Morris, *John P. Holland,* 109; O'Grady, "Irish-Americans and Anglo-American Relations," 12–13.

18. Ward, *Ireland and Anglo-American Relations,* 1–18.

19. Beckett, *The Making of Modern Ireland,* 411–24.

20. George E. Mowry, *The Era of Theodore Roosevelt and the Birth of Modern America: 1900–1912;* Arthur S. Link, *Woodrow Wilson and the Progressive Era: 1910–1917* (New York: Harper & Row, 1954), 1–24.

CHAPTER 9

1. Beckett, *The Making of Modern Ireland,* 424–34.

2. Tansill, *America and the Fight for Irish Freedom,* 121; Ward, *Ireland and Anglo-American Relations* 7–29.

3. Wittke, *Irish in America,* 168–171; 212–14, 279–84.

4. Austin J. App, "The Germans," in *The Immigrants' Influence on Wilson's Peace Policies*, ed. by Joseph P. O'Grady (Lexington: University of Kentucky Press, 1967), 31; Devoy, *Recollections*, 391–484.

5. Dean R. Esslinger, "American, German and Irish Attitudes Toward Neutrality, 1914–1917; A Study of Catholic Minorities," *Catholic Historical Review*, LIII (1967), 194–216; Edward Cuddy, "Irish-Americans, Propagandists and American Neutrality, 1914–1917," *Mid-America*, XLIX (1967), 252–75.

6. Beckett, *The Making of Modern Ireland*, 426–441; Costigan, *A History of Modern Ireland*, 304–30.

7. William M. Leary, Jr., "Woodrow Wilson, Irish-Americans and the Election of 1916," *Journal of American History*, LIV (1967), 57–72.

8. Ward, *Ireland and Anglo-American Relations*, 128–41.

9. Wittke, *Irish in America*, 283–285.

10. Quoted in Joseph P. O'Grady, "The Irish," in *The Immigrants' Influence*, 57–58.

11. Tansill, *America and the Fight for Irish Freedom*, 241. Representatives McLenore, Mason of Illinois and Champ Clark (in Devoy's words, "a friend of Ireland" (see *Gaelic-American*, January 19, 1918) met Mrs. Skiffington and served as her guide through political Washington. See also John Duff, "The Versailles Treaty and the Irish-Americans," *Journal of American History*, LV (December, 1968).

12. Philadelphia *Irish Press*, March 23, April 6, 1918; *Gaelic-American*, March 23, April 6 and 13, 1918. In spite of these meetings and the resolutions before Congress, Representative Flood, according to the *Irish Press*, April 6, 1918, stated "that he has heard of no public demand on behalf of Ireland" which caused some concern to Mr. McGarrity. See Tansill, *America and Irish Freedom*, 271.

13. O'Grady, "The Irish," 61–62; *Irish Press*, July 13, October 12, 1918; *Gaelic-American*, October 22, 1918. All of these events received wide coverage in the Irish-American press.

14. *Irish Press*, October 26, 1918; *Gaelic-American*, November 2, 1918.

15. Tansill, *America and Irish Freedom*, 280, 291; *Gaelic-American*, December 14, 1918.

16. Ward, *Ireland and Anglo-American Relations*, 166–67.

17. James P. Walsh, "De Valera in the United States, 1919," *Records* (of the American Catholic Historical Society of Philadelphia) LXXIII (1962), 94; John Tracey Ellis, *The Life of James Cardinal Gibbons*, 2 vols. (1952), 11, 226. Gibbons usually took a moderate course on this particular question, and his biographer did not feel that this speech at the Irish Race Convention changed this. It would seem from the newspaper accounts, however, that Gibbons in 1919 was not as restrained as Ellis claims he was. Tansill, *America and Irish Freedom*, 301; Seth P. Tillman, *Anglo-American*

Relations at the Peace Conference, 1919 (Princeton: Princeton University Press, 1961), 198.

18. *Irish Press*, February 22, March 23, 1918; Tansill, *America and Irish Freedom*, 308; Tillman, *Anglo-American Relations*, 198; *Congressional Record*, 65th Congress, 3rd Session, 5027–57.

19. Tansill, *America and Irish Freedom*, 310.

20. Bailey, *Woodrow Wilson and the Great Betrayal*, 27, claims that he wanted to tell them to "go to hell," but Tansill, *America and Irish Freedom*, 313, 316, 319, claims he did not because he needed their votes. There is no indication that Wilson acted for that reason. Tillman, *Anglo-American Relations*, 200.

21. *Congressional Record*, 66th Congress, 1st Session, Part I, 393, 671, 1374, 1727.

22. Quoted in Tansill, *America and Irish Freedom*, 319.

23. *Irish Press*, May 24, 1919; Tansill, *America and Irish Freedom*, 328.

24. *Congressional Record*, 66th Congress, 1st Session, Part I, 729.

25. Tansill, *America and Irish Freedom*, 332. Tansill is especially useful when it comes to the work of Cohalan and the Friends of Irish Freedom, mainly because he had access to Cohalan's personal papers.

26. Walsh, "De Valéra" 96. Walsh claims that "the mathematics professor" in the speech in Chicago "put a stop to this behavior," that is, the Irish-American effort to use his visit to stir up opposition to the League and Wilson's treaty. Yet on page 101, he shows how Hearst used De Valéra's visit to do just this and later, how De Valéra himself declared against the League. There are some obvious errors in this article, but it does give some indications of how San Francisco received him and how the Catholic clergy used De Valéra to arouse Catholic opposition to the league.

27. *Congressional Record*, 66th Congress, 1st Session, Part I, 496, 729; *Irish Press*, June 21, July 5, 1919. In every issue this argument appeared in the course of battle. Tansill, *America and Irish Freedom*, 331; *The News Letter*, October 10, 1919. This was published weekly in Washington by the Irish National Bureau, the lobbying arm of the Friends of Irish Freedom, beginning in the summer of 1919 and carrying beyond the second defeat of the treaty.

28. *Congressional Record*, 66th Congress, 1st Session, Part 2, 1781, 2077; Part 5, 4651–4718.

29. *Ibid.*, Part 7, 7048, 7156.

30. Tansill, *America and Irish Freedom*, 338.

31. For the story of the Black and Tans, see Edgar Holt, *Protest in Arms: The Irish Troubles, 1916–1923* (London: Putnam and Sons, 1960).

32. *Irish Press*, December 6, 20, 1919, January 31, February 14, March 13, 1920.

33. *Congressional Record*, 66th Congress, 2nd Session, Part 5, 4522 The debate carried from page 4492 to page 4522.

34. *Ibid.*, Part 8, 7767; Part 8, 8673; Part 9, 9293. *Irish Press*, December 6, 1919; *Gaelic-American*, December 19, 21, 1919; *The News Letter* December 19, 1919.

35. Ward, *Ireland and Anglo-American Relations*, 221–25, 229.

36. For these details, see Beckett, *Making of Modern Ireland*, 475–78 and Francis X. Carroll, "The Irish Question in Anglo-American Relations 1919–1923," paper used in the Maurice Francis Egan Lectures, La Salle College, October 28, 1970.

CHAPTER 10

1. Costigan, *Modern Ireland*, 357–58; Robert A. Divine, *American Immigration Policy, 1924–1952* (New Haven: Yale University Press, 1957), 26–51; Jethro K. Lieberman, *Are Americans Extinct?* (New York: Wallser and Company, 1968), 188–89; Wittke, *We Who Built America*, 531–33.

2. Wittke, *The Irish in America*, 292–94. The question of housing changes since 1920 is open to study, but it seems clear that since 1920 the Irish have participated in this American experience. For an example see Andrew M. Greeley, *That Most Distressful Nation* (Chicago: Quadrangle Books, 1972), 181, 231–246.

3. This fact may help to explain the problem of the Catholic failure to produce intellectuals in the twentieth century. See Thomas E. O'Dea, *American Catholic Dilemma* (New York: Sheed and Ward, 1958).

4. It would appear the Irish still play a role in police departments. Patrick Murphy has in 1971 succeeded Howard Leary in New York's Department. In the years before World War II the Irish played a prominent role in the ranks of New York's teachers, but in the last twenty years they have lost that place to Jewish-Americans. Yet in Philadelphia a Sullivan and a Ryan led the local chapter of the A.F.L.

5. The theme of this paragraph rests upon a number of conversations with first- and second-generation Irishmen.

6. Any current issue of a Catholic publication will confirm this. A search of the latest editions of N. W. Ayer's *Newspaper Directory* also tells the changing situation. The current situation in Northern Ireland, however, may have caused a change. A new paper *The Forthnightly* is now being published in Massachusetts.

7. The problem of the O.A.H. is clear in many cities. One such club in Philadelphia no longer has an outside sign. Every time the officers erect one, Negro youths destroy it. The club itself, thus, lingers in a state of limbo or semiretirement.

8. This is again based upon personal experience and a series of conversations.

9. For the full story see Charles Tull, *Father Coughlin and the New Deal* (Syracuse: Syracuse University Press, 1965).

10. Shannon, *The American Irish*, 319–326.

11. The recent death of Richard Cardinal Cushing comes just as the Irish are moving out of Boston. Coupled to John McCormick's retirement from Congress in 1970, it may well mark the end of the Irish in Boston.

12. My guess would be that the latter would prove more likely. For some background on this question see the study by O'Dea mentioned above and John Tracy Ellis, *American Catholicism*, 2nd ed., rev. (Chicago: University of Chicago Press, 1969), 148–51. Greeley gives additional evidence in his *That Most Distressful Nation*, 187–190, 204–206.

13. Shannon, *The American Irish*, 261–81.

14. The Kennedy family is only the more noticeable. Most American cities today have similar examples.

15. See *Biographical Directory of Congress*, 1675, 1971; Don Lahbuck, *Patrick J. Hurley* (New York: Henry Regency Company, 1956), 65, 74, 84–120; Link, *Woodrow Wilson and the Progressive Era*, 65.

16. For the story of Smith see H. F. Pringle, *Alfred E. Smith* (New York: Mary Asius, 1927); Oscar Handlin, *Al Smith and His America* (Boston: Little Brown & Company, 1958); Edmund A. Moore, *A Catholic Runs For President: The Campaign of 1928* (Boston: Little, Brown, 1956).

17. Shannon, *The American Irish*, 327, argues that the New Deal marked a great opportunity for Irish politicians, but I would argue that they had greater opportunities in the period of great excitement in Ireland.

18. One view of Truman's problems can be found in Jules Abels, *The Truman Scandals* (Chicago: Henry Regency, 1956) which is critical of McGrath's role.

19. Dwight D. Eisenhower, *Mandate For Change, 1953–1956* (New York: Doubleday, 1963), 127–128, 355 indicates that Herbert Brownell suggested Durkin and Charles Wilson suggested Mitchell.

20. This may be too harsh on Curley as I have a certain regard for his brand of Robin Hood politics, but I am afraid it is close to the truth.

21. Senator McCarthy's career has generated a heavy literature which has shown few signs of abating. For a short evaluation of his life, see Shannon, *The American Irish*, Chapter 18. Longer studies can be found in Richard H. Rovere, *Senator Joe McCarthy* (London: Methuen and Company, 1957), and William F. Buckley, Jr. and L. B. Bozell, *McCarthy and His Enemies* (Chicago: Henry Regency, 1954).

22. Edward M. Levine, *The Irish and Irish Politicians* (Notre Dame:

University of Notre Dame, 1966), 109–202; Theodore H. White, *The Making of the President 1960* (New York: Atheneum, 1961), Chapter 2.

23. Theodore C. Sorensen, *Kennedy* (New York: Harper & Row, 1965), 79–86.

24. For a discussion of this see Andrew Greeley, *That Most Distressful Nation*, 248, 255, 262–270.

25. The story of the Civil Rights Movement in Mother Ireland is too near for the historian to offer any kind of adequate analysis as far as its impact upon the American Irish is concerned. The movement itself, however, has been described in numerous articles in the popular journals and in the press. Much has been made of American support for the IRA movement, but my conversations with various Irish-Americans would lead me to believe that this is highly exaggerated. For the future of the IRA see Dennis Clark, "What Way the I.R.A.?" *Commonweal* (January 5, 1973) 294–297.

26. Greeley, *That Most Distressful Nation*, xxvi.

Glossary

The Act of Union of 1801. This act dissolved the Irish Parliament and gave seats in the British Parliament to representatives from Ireland.

American Land League. The American branch of the Irish National Land League which flourished in the early 1880's.

Ancient Order of Hibernians. Most powerful voice of Irish-America in the first two decades of the twentieth century.

Anglo-Irish Ascendancy. The transplanted Protestant landowning class of Ireland in the eighteenth and nineteenth centuries.

Anglo-Irish. Gaelicized descendants of the old Anglo-Normans who gradually became more Irish than English.

Anglo-Normans. English conquerors of Ireland in the twelfth century.

Auxiliaries. A special elite force of ex-officers of the British army that was introduced into Ireland in 1919 and fought the IRA.

Brian Baru. The first truly high king of Ireland and victor at the Battle of Contarf in 1014.

Black and Tans. British forces in Ireland during the crisis in 1919–20, composed of unemployed veterans of World War I.

William Borah. United States senator who appealed to the Irish vote in his drive to defeat the League of Nations in 1919–20.

Roger Casement. Irish hero who served as the link between German leaders and the Irish revolutionaries of 1916.

James Carey. The informer in the Phoenix Park murder case of 1883.

Mathew Carey. Prominent Irish-American bookseller and printer in the late eighteenth century.

Edmond Carson. Leader of the Protestant Irish in Ulster before and during World War I.

The Catholic Association. Organization Daniel O'Connell created in the 1820's to fight for the right of Catholics to hold political office.

Clan-na-Gael. Irish-American organization founded in the late 1860's as the successor to the Fenian movement.

Richard FitzGilbert de Clare. The Earl of Pembroke, who led the Anglo-Norman invasion of Ireland. Also known as "Strongbow."

Patrick Cleburne. Irish-American Confederate general from Alabama.

Daniel Cohalan. Along with John Devoy, he rebuilt the Clan-na-Gael in the first two decades of the twentieth century as a powerful voice in radical Irish-American circles.

Patrick Collins. Long-time Irish-Catholic politician in Boston.

Michael Corcoran. Commander of Fighting Sixty-ninth during the Civil War.

Charles Coughlin. Radio priest of America during the 1930's.

Richard Croker. First Irish-born boss of Tammany Hall.

James Curley. Irish-Catholic politician from Boston.

Richard Cardinal Cushing. Irish-Catholic cardinal of Boston and friend of the Kennedy family.

Eamon De Valera. American-born Irish hero of the Easter Rebellion and later president of Ireland.

John Devoy. A Fenian of the 1860's and long-time leader of the Clan-na-Gael.

Michael Davitt. Founder of the Land League.

"Wild Bill" Donovan. Commander of the Fighting Sixty-ninth during World War I.

Maurice France Egan. A prominent Irish-Catholic who served on many diplomatic missions for Theodore Roosevelt.

Patrick Egan. Treasurer of the National Land League and later American minister to Chile.

Robert Emmet. An Irish revolutionary executed in 1803 whose famous "Speech on the Dock" inspired the Irish in their fight for independence.

James Farley. Irish-American manager of Franklin Roosevelt's 1932 presidential campaign.

Fenian Brotherhood. The American branch of the Irish Revolutionary Brotherhood in the 1860's.

Fighting Sixty-ninth. The Irish regiment of New York Volunteers in the Civil War and in World War I.

John Finerty. An Irish-American congressman from Chicago and publisher of the Irish paper, *Chicago Citizen*.

Patrick Ford. Founder of the New York *Irish World*, the most influential Irish paper in America in the late nineteenth century.

Friends of Irish Freedom. The organization Devoy and Cohalan formed to pressure America into giving Ireland her freedom at the end of World War II.

James Cardinal Gibbon. The dominant Irish Catholic churchman in America from 1885 to his death in 1921.

William Gladstone. Prime minister of England and friend of Ireland in the 1880's and 1890's.

Michael Glennon. Successor to Anthony M. Keiley as president of the I.C.B.U. and prominent Democrat in Norfolk, Virginia.

Franklin B. Gowan. President of the Reading Railroad during the Molly Maguires disturbances.

Henry Grattan. Leader of Ireland's Protestant nationalism in the last half of the eighteenth century.

Martin I. J. Griffin. Long-time secretary of the I.C.B.U. and editor of its *Journal.*

Arthur Griffith. Founder of the Sinn Fein party in Ireland.

William C. Grace. First Catholic mayor of New York in 1880.

William J. Harrity. An early graduate of La Salle College and the first Catholic to serve as chairman of the National Democratic Committee in 1892.

John P. Holland. Inventor of the first operational submarine in the U.S. Navy.

John Hughes. Irish-Catholic archbishop of New York during the national period of the 1840's and 1850's.

Douglas Hyde. Founder of the Gaelic League in Ireland.

"Invincibles." A radical Irish group who saw physical force as the solution to Ireland's problems during the 1880's.

Irish Catholic Benevolent Union. The most powerful Irish voice in the country in the 1870's and 1880's.

The Irish National League of America. The American branch of Charles Stewart Parnell's National League.

Irish Republican Army. The force that fought for Irish freedom under Michael Collins at the end of World War I and which has continued to fight the British army in Ulster in 1972.

Anthony M. Keiley. Long-time president of the I.C.B.U. and prominent Democratic politician in Virginia.

"Honest John" Kelly. Successor of William Tweed as "boss" of Tammany in the 1870's and 1880's.

John Keogh. A Catholic leader in the 1790's who led the fight against the Penal Code.

Kilmanham Pact. An agreement between William Gladstone and Charles S. Parnell that ended the land agitation in Ireland in the summer of 1882.

Know-Nothings. Anti-Catholic and anti-immigrant political party of the 1850's.

John Krol. The Polish-American cardinal of Philadelphia in the 1960's.

Joseph McCarthy. Irish-Catholic Republican senator of the 1950's.

J. Howard McGrath. The Irish politician from Rhode Island who served as Truman's attorney-general.

Peter J. McGuire. The father of Labor Day.

James McParlan. Irish-Catholic informer from the Pinkerton National Detective Agency who infiltrated the Molly Maguires.

Thomas Meagher. A "Young Irelander" of 1848 and a Civil War Union general.

Molly Maguires. A group of Irish-Catholic coal miners who used terror tactics against the coal-mine owners in the late 1860's and 1870's.

Patrick Moore. Irish-Catholic commanding general of the First Regiment Infantry, Virginia Volunteers.

Charles Murphy. Irish "boss" of Tammany Hall who wanted Al Smith elected president of the United States.

National Land League. The creation of Michael Davitt and Charles S. Parnell which fought for land reform in Ireland in the early 1880's.

National League. Charles S Parnell's organization which took the place of the National Land League in 1883.

Michael J. O'Brien. Historian of the American-Irish Historical Society.

Daniel O'Connell. "King of the Beggars" who led the movement for Catholic emancipation and repeal of the Act of Union in Ireland during the 1820's through the 1840's.

James O'Donnell. An Irishman who claimed American citizenship after he had murdered James Carey, the informer in the Phoenix Park murder case.

John O'Hara. Archbishop and cardinal of Philadelphia in the 1950's.

Jeremiah O'Leary. Leader of the American Truth Society and anti-Woodrow Wilson Irish-American.

John O'Mahoney. Founder of the Fenians, the American branch of the Irish Revolutionary Brotherhood during the 1800's.

Hugh O'Neill. The Earl of Tyrone, who led the battle against Elizabeth I's attempts to suppress Ulster and who went into exile in 1603.

John Boyle O'Reilly. The Fenian poet and editor of the Boston *Pilot*.

The Pale. The area around Dublin which represented the only area of effective English control in the fifteenth and sixteenth centuries.

Charles Stewart Parnell. The Protestant descendant of the Anglo-Irish Ascendency who led the Irish Catholics during the 1880's in their struggles against the Irish land system and for Home Rule.

Sir Robert Peel. The prime minister of England during the Great Famine.

Penal Laws. British laws that denied Irish Catholics many civil, religious, and personal rights during the eighteenth century.

John Redmond. Leader of the Home Rule party in the British Parliament during the 1890's and into World War I.

Repeal Association. The organization Daniel O'Connell created to force the repeal of the Act of Union.

William Roberts. Leader of the senate faction of the Fenian movement in the late 1860's and later congressman and minister to Chile.

P. J. Sheridan. An Irishman who resided in America who was accused of belonging to the radical Irish group known as the "Invincible."

Philip H. Sheridan. A second-generation Irish-Catholic Union general.

Alfred Smith. Irish Tammany politician who ran for the presidency in 1920.

James Stephens. Founder of the Irish Revolutionary Brotherhood in Dublin.

Alexander Sullivan. A leader of the "Triangle" which controlled the Clan-na-Gael in the mid-1880's.

Treaty of Limerick, 1691. This ended the struggle between William of Orange and James II for control of Ireland.

James Tynan. The alleged "Number One" of the "Invincibles" who resided in America.

Vinegar Hill. The site of an Irish defeat during the Revolution of 1798.

Frank P. Walsh. Chairman of the American Commission for Irish Independence.

Frederick Wood. Catholic bishop of Philadelphia in the 1860's during the Molly Maguire disturbances.

Young Irelanders. The Irish Revolutionaries of 1848.

A Bibliographic Essay

The printed materials on the history of Ireland and her people are, of course, quite extensive and that on the Irish in America is not that far behind, which may surprise many. To read all that is available would appeal to few readers of this book. Thus, what follows is merely a guide to that material, and only a beginner's guide at that. Because the student of Irish-America must first have a fine grounding in Irish history, books on the latter will be mentioned first.

Anyone who wishes to know more about the Irish should start with T. W. Moody and F. X. Martin, eds., *The Course of Irish History* (New York: Weybright and Talley, 1967), even though at times the writing is pedantic and the story thin. A more readable survey would be Giovanni Costigan, *A History of Modern Ireland* (New York: Pegasus, 1970). These could be supplemented by the still standard text, Edmund Curtis, *The History of Ireland*, 6th ed. (London: Methuen, 1965 reprint). The Middle Ages are more than adequately covered in a great book, A. J. Otway-Ruthveu, *A History of Medieval Ireland* (London: Ernest Benn, 1968), while J. C. Beckett, *The Making of Modern Ireland, 1603–1923* (London: Faber and Faber, 1966), surveys the modern period in great detail in a great book.

For the seventeenth and eighteenth centuries one must read the works by John G. Simms, of which *Jacobite Ireland, 1865–1691* (London: Routledge and Kegan Paul, 1969) is the latest, and Maureen Wall, especially her *The Penal Laws, 1687–1780: Church and State from the Treaty of Limerick to the Accession of George III* (Dundale: Dublin Historical Association, 1961). The material for the last half of the eighteenth century is also enormous, but one should not fail to read the now somewhat older study by Stephen Gwynn, *Henry Grattan and His Times* (London: Brown and Nolan, 1939). The bibliographies in *The Course of Irish History* and *The Making of Modern Ireland* are helpful for additional reading here.

For Ireland the nineteenth century brought events of enormous significance. Numerous books can be found on Daniel O'Connell, but one should begin with the reading of Sean O'Faolain, *King of the Beggars* (New York: Viking Press, 1938). The Famine period calls to mind Cecil Woodham-Smith's study *The Great Hunger* (New York: Harper & Row,

[179]

1962) and *The Great Famine: Studies in Irish History, 1845–52* (New York: New York University Press, 1957), ed. by R. D. Edwards and T. D. Williams. Anyone interested in the 1850's and 1860's has to read Desmond Ryan, *The Fenian Chief: A Biography of James Stephens* (Coral Gables: University of Miami Press, 1969), while David Thornley's *Issac Butt and Home Rule* (London: Maggilihan and Kee, 1964) introduces the next great movement. Charles S. Parnell has been the subject of far too many books to mention here, but the best of the recent studies for him and his period are Conor C. O'Brien, *Parnell and His Party: 1880–1890* (Oxford: The Clarendon Press, 1957) and Francis Lyons, *The Fall of Parnell, 1890–91* (London: Routledge and Kegan Paul, 1960). Both of these studies have excellent bibliographies for this period. Another excellent study of the Parnell years is J. L. Hammond, *Gladstone and the Irish Nation* (London: Longmans Green, 1938). Michael Davitt still needs a full-scale biographer, as Francis Sheeky-Skeffington's *Michael Davitt* (London: MacGibbon & Kee, 1967 reprint) is not adequate. T.W. Moody is, at the time of this writing, engaged in a study of this major figure in Irish politics. In the meantime one should read Davitt's own book, *The Fall of Federalism in Ireland* (New York: Harper & Brothers, 1904).

The post-Parnell period brought some peace and quiet to Ireland, but it also brought with it a feverish organizational activity. A good survey of these years can be found in C. Cruise O'Brien, *The Shaping of Modern Ireland* (London: Routledge and Kegan Paul, 1960). One should also read some of the biographies of the various leading figures of this period. The Easter Week rebellion has produced a series of books. For a good selection of these for the beginner see the bibliography at the end of *The Course of Irish History*. One book that must be read for this period is Tom B. Barry, *Guerrila Days in Ireland* (Dublin: Irish Press, 1949). The struggles after independence are told in Callon Younger, *Ireland's Civil War* (London: Millers, 1968). One version of the Irish Republican Army can be found in J. Bell, *The Secret Army: The I.R.A., 1916–1970* (New York: John Day, 1971). Morley Ayreast's *The Republic of Ireland* (New York: New York University Press, 1970) is the latest on the general study of the nation since independence.

Once the reader gains the full view of Irish history and its problems he might want to analyze the general problem of immigration in America first, before moving into the detailed study of the Irish. Maldwy Allen Jones, *American Immigration* (Chicago: University of Chicago Press, 1960) and Carl Wittke's, *We Who Built America*, rev. ed. (Cleveland: Press of the Case Western Reserve University, 1967).

For the Irish in particular one should start with Wittke's *The Irish in America* (Baton Rouge: Louisiana State University Press, 1956) which is an encyclopedia of information on the Irish in this country. William V. Shannon has taken a different approach in *The American Irish* (New York:

Macmillan, 1963). For those who came before 1800, H. J. Ford, *The Scotch-Irish in America* (Princeton: Princeton University Press, 1915), tells the story, but he should be read in conjunction with James G. Leyburn, *The Scotch-Irish: A Social History* (Chapel Hill: University of North Carolina Press, 1962). The period from the Napoleonic Wars to the Famine is covered in W. F. Adams, *Ireland and Irish Emigration to the New World from 1815 to the Famine* (New Haven: Yale University Press, 1932). The best story of what happened to the famine Irish once they got here is T. N. Brown, *Irish-American Nationalism* (Philadelphia: Lippincott, 1966). William D'Arcy, *The Fenian Movement in the United States, 1858–1886* (Washington: The Catholic University of America Press, 1947) still remains the basic study for this question. For the Irish in Boston one has to read Oscar Handlin, *Boston's Immigrants, 1790–1880*, David and Olney, eds. (Cambridge: Harvard University Press, 1959) while Florence S. Gibson's *The Attitude of the New York Irish Toward State and National Affairs, 1848–92* (New York: Columbia University Press, 1951) is an excellent source of Irish reactions to a wide spectrum of events. J. McCayne described the draft riots in New York in his *The Second Rebellion* (New York: The Deal Press, 1968), and Joseph M. Hernon gives an interesting view of Ireland's interest in the American Civil War in his *Celts, Catholic and Copperheads: Ireland Views the American Civil War* (Columbus: Ohio State University Press, 1968).

The post-Civil War years produced a number of strong national organizations. The best studies of these are Joan Marie Donohue, *The Irish Catholic Benevolent Union* (Washington: The Catholic University of America Press, 1953); Joan Bland, *The Hibernian Crusade* (Washington: The Catholic University of America Press, 1951); and the extensive John O'Dea, *History of the Ancient Order of Hibernians and Ladies Auxiliary*, 4 vols. (Philadelphia: The Ancient Order of Hibernians, 1923). There are also a number of studies of local groups. One that should be read is Richard C. Murphy and Lawrence J. Mannion, *The History of the Friendly Sons of Saint Patrick in the City of New York* (New York: J. C. Dillon, 1962), and W. G. Broehl's *The Molly Maguires* (Cambridge: Harvard University Press, 1964) cannot be missed.

For the 1880's one has to read James J. Roche, *The Life of John Boyle O'Reilly* (New York: The Mershan Co., 1891) and M. P. Curran, *The Life of Patrick A. Collins* (Norwood: Henry Bill, 1904). The story of the link between the Irish and Anglo-American relations can be found in two unpublished dissertations, Joseph P. O'Grady, "Irish-American and Anglo-American Relations, 1880–1888" (University of Pennsylvania, 1965), and Edward A. Jameson, "Irish Americans, The Irish Question and American Diplomacy, 1895–1921" (Harvard University, 1944) as well as in Alan J. Ward's *Ireland and Anglo-American Relations, 1899–1921* (London: London School of Economics, 1969). Another study by Charles Tansill,

America and the Fight for Irish Freedom (New York: Devan-Adair, 1957), must be used with care.

The Irish impact upon the church, of course, can be seen in John Tracy Ellis, *American Catholics*, 2nd ed. (Chicago: University of Chicago Press, 1969) and in T. T. MacAvoy, *A History of the Catholic Church in the United States* (South Bend: University of Notre Dame Press, 1969).

The world of Irish-American studies has a number of memoirs and personal stories, but one cannot avoid reading John Devoy, *Recollections of an Irish Rebel* (New York: Charles P. Young, 1929) as there is nothing comparable.

For the years after 1920, the story of Irish-Americans can be found in the biographies of their political leaders and in the short studies of the literary figures. The works of James T. Farrell, the triology of *Studs Lonigan* and Danny O'Neill, best tell what life was like for the average Irishman in America. For the story of the Irish in Chicago see Edward M. Levine, *The Irish and Irish Politicians* (Notre Dame: University of Notre Dame, 1966) while Daniel P. Moynihan's chapter on the Irish in Nathan Glazer and Daniel P. Moynihan, *Beyond the Melting Pot*, rev. ed. (Cambridge: M.I.T. Press, 1970) tells the story of the Irish in New York. Dr. Dennis Clark is now completing a study of the Irish in Philadelphia which will be published by Temple University Press. Father Andrew Greeley has a number of interesting articles dealing with the Irish in the 1960's. See his articles "The Last of the American Irish Fade Away," *New York Times Magazine*, March 14, 1971 and "The American Irish Since the Death of Studs Lonigan," *The Critic*, May-June, 1971, 27-33. He has taken these and some others, and added to them to produce his book *That Most Distressful Nation: The Taming of the American Irish* (Chicago: Quadrangle Books, 1972). Many will disagree with his views on the Irish that are contained there, but it is a provocative study.

Index

183